Exclusive Online Res

As our valued reader, your purchase of this book includes access to exclusive online resources designed to enhance your learning experience. These resources can be downloaded from our website, www.vibrantpublishers.com, and are created to help you apply Business Intelligence concepts effectively.

Online resources for this book include the following five essential templates:

- Business Intelligence Project Roadmap Template
- Business Intelligence Requirements Gathering Form
- Data Quality Assessment Worksheet
- Business Intelligence Tool Evaluation Matrix
- Business Intelligence Performance Metrics Tracker

Why these online resources are valuable:

- **Practical application:** The ready-to-use templates simplify complex business intelligence processes.

- **Step-by-step guidance:** They enable a clear understanding of concepts, efficient implementation of techniques, and skill refinement.

- **Enhanced learning experience:** They reinforce knowledge with structured worksheets, evaluation matrices, and performance-tracking tools.

How to access your online resources:

1. **Visit the website:** Go to www.vibrantpublishers.com

2. **Find your book:** Navigate to the book's product page via the "Shop" menu or by searching for the book title in the search bar.

3. **Request the resources:** Scroll down to the "Request Sample Book/Online Resource" section.

4. **Enter your details:** Enter your preferred email ID and select "Online Resource" as the resource type. Lastly, select "User Type" and submit the request.

5. **Check your inbox:** The resources will be delivered directly to your email.

Alternatively, for quick access: simply scan the QR code below to go directly to the product page and request the online resources by filling in the required details.

bit.ly/bi-slm

Happy learning!

SELF-LEARNING MANAGEMENT SERIES

VIBRANT
PUBLISHERS

BUSINESS INTELLIGENCE ESSENTIALS

YOU ALWAYS WANTED TO KNOW

Demystifying data analytics
for smarter business decisions

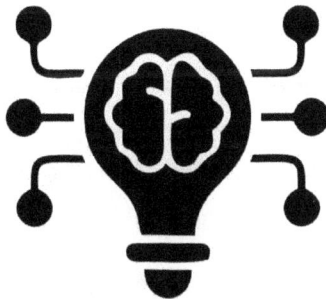

IRENE TOBAJAS

BUSINESS INTELLIGENCE ESSENTIALS YOU ALWAYS WANTED TO KNOW

First Edition

Paperback ISBN 10: 1-63651-336-0
Paperback ISBN 13: 978-1-63651-336-2

Ebook ISBN 10: 1-63651-337-9
Ebook ISBN 13: 978-1-63651-337-9

Hardback ISBN 10: 1-63651-338-7
Hardback ISBN 13: 978-1-63651-338-6

Library of Congress Control Number: 2024951291

This publication is designed to provide accurate and authoritative information in regard to the subject matter covered. The Author has made every effort in the preparation of this book to ensure the accuracy of the information. However, information in this book is sold without warranty either expressed or implied. The Author or the Publisher will not be liable for any damages caused or alleged to be caused either directly or indirectly by this book.

Vibrant Publishers books are available at special quantity discount for sales promotions, or for use in corporate training programs. For more information please write to bulkorders@vibrantpublishers.com

Please email feedback / corrections (technical, grammatical or spelling) to spellerrors@vibrantpublishers.com

To access the complete catalogue of Vibrant Publishers, visit www.vibrantpublishers.com

SELF-LEARNING MANAGEMENT SERIES

TITLE	PAPERBACK* ISBN

BUSINESS AND ENTREPRENEURSHIP

BUSINESS COMMUNICATION ESSENTIALS	9781636511634
BUSINESS ETHICS ESSENTIALS	9781636513324
BUSINESS LAW ESSENTIALS	9781636511702
BUSINESS PLAN ESSENTIALS	9781636511214
BUSINESS STRATEGY ESSENTIALS	9781949395778
ENTREPRENEURSHIP ESSENTIALS	9781636511603
INTERNATIONAL BUSINESS ESSENTIALS	9781636513294
PRINCIPLES OF MANAGEMENT ESSENTIALS	9781636511542

COMPUTER SCIENCE AND TECHNOLOGY

BLOCKCHAIN ESSENTIALS	9781636513003
MACHINE LEARNING ESSENTIALS	9781636513775
PYTHON ESSENTIALS	9781636512938

DATA SCIENCE FOR BUSINESS

BUSINESS INTELLIGENCE ESSENTIALS	9781636513362
DATA ANALYTICS ESSENTIALS	9781636511184

FINANCIAL LITERACY AND ECONOMICS

COST ACCOUNTING & MANAGEMENT ESSENTIALS	9781636511030
FINANCIAL ACCOUNTING ESSENTIALS	9781636510972
FINANCIAL MANAGEMENT ESSENTIALS	9781636511009
MACROECONOMICS ESSENTIALS	9781636511818
MICROECONOMICS ESSENTIALS	9781636511153
PERSONAL FINANCE ESSENTIALS	9781636511849

*Also available in Hardback & Ebook formats

SELF-LEARNING MANAGEMENT SERIES

TITLE	PAPERBACK* ISBN

HUMAN RESOURCE AND ORGANIZATIONAL SUCCESS

DIVERSITY, EQUITY, AND INCLUSION ESSENTIALS	9781636512976
DIVERSITY IN THE WORKPLACE ESSENTIALS	9781636511122
HR ANALYTICS ESSENTIALS	9781636510347
HUMAN RESOURCE MANAGEMENT ESSENTIALS	9781949395839
ORGANIZATIONAL BEHAVIOR ESSENTIALS	9781636512303
ORGANIZATIONAL DEVELOPMENT ESSENTIALS	9781636511481

LEADERSHIP AND PERSONAL DEVELOPMENT

DECISION MAKING ESSENTIALS	9781636510026
INDIA'S ROAD TO TRANSFORMATION: WHY LEADERSHIP MATTERS	9781636512273
LEADERSHIP ESSENTIALS	9781636510316
TIME MANAGEMENT ESSENTIALS	9781636511665

MODERN MARKETING AND SALES

CONSUMER BEHAVIOR ESSENTIALS	9781636513263
DIGITAL MARKETING ESSENTIALS	9781949395747
MARKETING MANAGEMENT ESSENTIALS	9781636511788
MARKET RESEARCH ESSENTIALS	9781636513744
SALES MANAGEMENT ESSENTIALS	9781636510743
SERVICES MARKETING ESSENTIALS	9781636511733
SOCIAL MEDIA MARKETING ESSENTIALS	9781636512181

*Also available in Hardback & Ebook formats

SELF-LEARNING MANAGEMENT SERIES

TITLE	PAPERBACK* ISBN

OPERATIONS AND PROJECT MANAGEMENT

AGILE ESSENTIALS	9781636510057
OPERATIONS & SUPPLY CHAIN MANAGEMENT ESSENTIALS	9781949395242
PROJECT MANAGEMENT ESSENTIALS	9781636510712
STAKEHOLDER ENGAGEMENT ESSENTIALS	9781636511511

CURRENT AFFAIRS

DIGITAL SHOCK	9781636513805

*Also available in Hardback & Ebook formats

This page is intentionally left blank

About the Author

Irene Tobajas is an accomplished Business Intelligence (BI) consultant with around a decade of experience in data analytics, operational excellence, and strategic decision-making. Irene's passion for data-driven strategies led her to establish her own consultancy, LUKiN Consulting, where she empowers businesses to optimize processes through effective BI implementation.

With a solid background in management consulting, Irene has helped renowned organizations such as Amazon, Veolia, and ArcelorMittal to leverage data for growth and innovation. Throughout her career, Irene has worked with clients across a wide range of industries, enabling them to transform complex data into actionable insights.

Irene's proficiency in tools like Tableau, Power BI, SQL, and advanced Excel equips her to craft impactful dashboards, interactive reports, and predictive models that drive organizational success. As a certified Continuous Improvement instructor, she excels at guiding teams through functions such as process reengineering, statistical analysis, decision modeling, and KPI/ dashboard reporting; embodying her passion for helping organizations turn complex data into actionable strategies.

Irene holds a Bachelor of Science (BSc Hons) degree in Business Management and has completed specialized training in BI, data visualization, and Lean methodologies. Over the years, Irene has developed a reputation for her hands-on, results-oriented approach. She is dedicated to simplifying Business Intelligence and making it accessible to professionals at all levels.

Her work emphasizes the integration of BI tools with real-world business challenges, empowering teams to leverage data and achieve their goals. When not consulting or writing, Irene enjoys exploring new trends in analytics and staying at the forefront of BI innovation. Her practical insights and deep understanding of BI have made her a sought-after expert in the field.

What experts say about this book!

"Business Intelligence Essentials" employs a clear, structured layout with readable fonts, enhancing technical content digestion. Its strength lies in comprehensive coverage of BI essentials—tools, analytics, implementation—paired with conversational language and practical examples, making complex concepts accessible.

Ideal for professionals, students, and mid-level managers seeking data-driven decision-making skills, it serves as a valuable resource for business analytics courses and organizational training programs. Libraries and startups would also benefit from its actionable insights for scalable BI strategies.

– Joyjit Pal, Strategy Consultant, Deloitte

"Business Intelligence Essentials You Always Wanted to Know" is a refreshingly practical guide, perfectly tailored for professionals, students, and business leaders looking to cut through the jargon and genuinely understand BI. The book does a great job simplifying complex concepts without sacrificing depth, and each chapter is thoughtfully designed to build foundational knowledge through real-world examples and clear explanations. Whether you're just starting your BI journey or looking to strengthen your strategic decision-making capabilities, this book provides actionable insights to confidently apply BI in real-world situations.

– Nicholas Kelly, Author of Delivering Data Analytics and How to Interpret Data, Creator of the Dashboard Wireframe Kit

What experts say about this book!

Business Intelligence (BI) has been a critical capability required by all serious organizations for decades, and will be so for decades to come. As the title suggests, this book describes the essential knowledge required to understand the fundamentals of BI. It is a perfect starting point on your learning journey towards becoming a BI professional. I wish I had this book when I was starting my career in data.

– Scott Ambler, Data Methodologist and Co-author of Refactoring Databases and Choose Your WoW!

The book is well laid out, easy to read, and easy to understand. It would provide a good introduction for newcomers to BI and for managers. I like the way each chapter started with a set of key learning objectives and ended with a quiz and a chapter summary. This would make the content useful for a course on these topics.

I also like the way she approaches projects by starting with the desired KPIs. What we find useful is mocking up some data with Excel or even Power BI Desktop to show users what we're talking about and to demonstrate the potential KPIs.

I liked the way the book leaned into prescriptive analytics as well. This is an area that so many books ignore. It was also good to see content on data governance and data quality.

– Dr. Greg Low, Consultant, Public Speaker, and Member of Microsoft RD Program in Australia

What experts say about this book!

At its core, Business Intelligence (BI) is about one thing—turning data into actionable insights. If you're in business today, you need BI. Whether you're making executive decisions, optimizing processes, or identifying trends, the ability to interpret and act on data is what separates thriving businesses from the ones that fall behind.

Business Intelligence Essentials You Always Wanted to Know does a great job of making this vast field digestible. The book walks readers through the essentials—data warehousing, ETL, analytics, dashboards—without getting lost in unnecessary jargon. The format is clean, the layout intuitive, and the concepts are explained with clarity. Expect practical examples, real-world applications, and a structured approach that moves from foundational knowledge to advanced BI techniques.

Who should read this? Students dipping their toes into business analytics, professionals looking to upskill, startup founders trying to make data-driven decisions, and mid-level managers who want to speak the language of data. It's also a handy addition to libraries and courses on business intelligence, data science, and information systems.

Some of the key areas it covers are: data fundamentals, visualization, strategy, and case studies. BI isn't just for data analysts anymore. It's for everyone who wants to make smarter decisions. This book lays the groundwork so that anyone—regardless of technical expertise—can understand and apply BI concepts effectively.

This book strips away the complexity of business intelligence and delivers a clear, structured guide for anyone looking to harness data for smarter decision-making. A must-read for professionals in today's data-driven world.

– Sireesha Pulipati, Analytics and BI Lead at Google
Author of Data Storytelling with Google Looker Studio

What experts say about this book!

Business Intelligence Essentials is an indispensable read for anyone looking to enter the Business Intelligence field. The book offers an engaging exploration of a wide range of topics, from basic analytics principles to the latest industry tools and technologies. One standout feature for me was the dedicated section on data storytelling — a vital yet often overlooked aspect in technical literature. This section is particularly well-presented, with clear explanations, illustrative figures, and practical examples that bring the concepts to life. Highly recommended!

– Nikhil Chhazed, Analytics & BI Manager, Amazon - Prime Video

This book provides a comprehensive introduction to the foundations of business intelligence, and more, with a self-learning format that is accessible and engaging. It is an excellent starting point for those new to BI. For those with experience in team or business management, it will serve as a reference book. Highly recommended for anyone looking to deepen their understanding of business intelligence.

– Pablo Carrera, Consulting Director, OMDIA

"Business Intelligence Essentials" is an insightful guide that clearly distinguishes Business Intelligence from Business Analytics and elaborates on the four types of analytics: descriptive, diagnostic, predictive, and prescriptive. The book effectively articulates these concepts in an enlightened manner. Chapters 8 and 9 are particularly valuable to me, offering practical advice on implementing and maintaining BI systems, with a strong focus on organisational change management. I will undoubtedly integrate this content into our World Class Manufacturing programme at ArcelorMittal.

– François Perlade, Head of Continuous Improvement, ArcelorMittal Tailored Blanks Europe

What experts say about this book!

This book offers a fantastic introduction to data and analytics—particularly the opening chapters, which lay a clear foundation for BI and how data teams operate. For anyone entering the field, it provides both a solid overview and detailed insights on advanced topics. It's ideal for professionals working in data and analytics or those simply wanting to build their data literacy. I'm definitely buying this for my team!

– Sharon Matthews, Head of Data & Analytics, Veolia - UK

Business Intelligence Essentials is a clear and accessible guide to understanding the world of BI and data analytics. From the fundamentals of BI systems to implementation and real-world examples, the book offers a structured tour through key tools, methodologies, and applications. With practical explanations of descriptive, predictive, and prescriptive analytics, it's an excellent read for anyone looking to make smarter, data-driven decisions.

– Iker Martínez de Soria Sánchez, Chief Digital Officer, PhD
City Hall - Getxo

This book cuts through the complexity of business intelligence with clarity and purpose, transforming information into insight, and insight into action. It prioritises learning over passive understanding, striking the right balance between technical depth and practical breadth.

– Natasha Sayce-Zelem, Director of Digital and Business Platform
Lloyds Banking Group

What experts say about this book!

As a leader of Business Intelligence teams throughout my career in Amazon and Procter & Gamble, I truly enjoyed this book by Irene Tobajas, and found it to be an exceptionally accessible yet comprehensive guide to BI. The book masterfully breaks down the components of modern Business Intelligence, and complements with practical chapter summaries and knowledge-testing quizzes as well as real-world examples of companies leveraging BI capabilities. Business Intelligence Essentials is an invaluable resource for both newcomers and experienced practitioners.

– Javier Rosales, Director of Product Strategy, Amazon - Fresh International

Table of Contents

This page is intentionally left blank

Acknowledgments

Writing *"Business Intelligence Essentials You Always Wanted to Know"* has been an extraordinary journey. There are so many people whose support and encouragement have made this book possible.

First and foremost, to my partner; I'm thankful for your unconditional support and for giving me the space to create and grow. Your guidance and genuine excitement for each little achievement made this process not only manageable but joyful. I could not have done it without you by my side.

To my sister, my biggest cheerleader and partner in all of my wild ideas. Thank you for believing in me and for being part of every adventure. Your faith in me has meant more than words can express.

To my mum, whose tireless dedication and love in raising me and my sister laid the foundation for everything I am today. Your strength and sacrifices have been my guiding light. Thank you for instilling in me the values and determination that have shaped my journey.

To my dad, thank you for your wisdom and endless stories. Your honesty and support have accompanied me through every major decision in my career. Your encouragement has always propelled me forward.

I am also deeply grateful to my friends and colleagues who have inspired me with their journeys and pushed me to do better. Your insights and shared experiences have enriched this book in countless ways. You know who you are, and I am so lucky to have you.

Of course, thank you to the Vibrant Publishers team, who from the very beginning placed their trust in me and gave me complete freedom to decide the contents of this book. Their continuous support and belief in my vision have been instrumental in bringing this project to life. Their guidance throughout this journey has been invaluable.

Finally, to the readers of this book, thank you for your curiosity and eagerness to learn. I hope this work empowers you as much as the journey of writing it has empowered me.

Preface

In today's fast-paced, data-centric world, the term "Business Intelligence" is everywhere. However, it symbolizes a lot more than a passing trend; it represents a transformative field that has revolutionized decision-making. This book is a culmination of my experiences, interactions within the professional field, and a deep desire to streamline what often appears complex or daunting to those unfamiliar with BI.

I came across BI very early in my career, where I directly observed how effectively presenting the right data could catalyze decisions and lead to remarkable business outcomes. Through collaborations with diverse teams and industries, I became aware of the challenges and opportunities that data presents. I discovered quickly that BI is not solely about numbers and software; it empowers individuals and organizations to navigate complexities clearly and act with purpose.

My professional journey has exposed me to various roles, from leading strategic projects and acting as CEOs' right hand, to focusing intensely on operational efficiency. These experiences have provided me with a unique understanding of how data can foster growth and innovation when utilized effectively. However, I also noticed a gap: many people found BI intimidating, or struggled to grasp its practical application. This realization became the motivation for writing this book.

My goal with *"Business Intelligence Essentials You Always Wanted to Know" (Business Intelligence Essentials)* is to make BI approachable and practical for everyone. Whether you are a manager seeking to enhance operations, an entrepreneur wanting to grasp market trends, or a data enthusiast discovering innovative methods to positively influence your organization, this book has you covered. I have filled this book with real-world examples, practical tips, and a structured approach to simplify complex concepts, enabling readers to quickly apply all the learnings from the book.

This book is dedicated to all those curious minds and decision-makers who understand that data is more than reports and dashboards; it's about empowering people, refining processes, and achieving strategic goals. I hope this book equips you with the knowledge and confidence to fully harness Business Intelligence and address your data challenges.

Introduction to the book

The ability to extract valuable insights from the information being generated non-stop around us, is crucial today. This skill presents both a challenge and an opportunity for companies. Businesses are investing a significant amount of resources to utilize this data and gain a competitive advantage. This effort helps improve efficiency and deliver greater value to their clients. This is indeed the point at which Business Intelligence becomes a treasured resource.

I would like to assure you that "Business Intelligence Essentials" is not just another conceptual manual on BI. My personal goal with this book is to equip you with the practical expertise and abilities to confidently implement BI in your initiatives, operations, and future strategies. Whether you are new to the field of BI or a seasoned expert looking to hone your skills, this book will provide you with a straight-forward and focused guide to the fundamentals of BI.

We will examine both essential and advanced BI concepts through practical examples, demonstrating BI's influence across various sectors. You will become both comfortable and confident with the BI lingo, as well as acquire the skills to gather, interpret and present data, and learn to transform it into tangible insights. By the time you finish the book, you will have the knowledge to comprehend and confidently apply BI solutions and optimize your team's data processes.

Here is a summary of what *Business Intelligence Essentials* will provide:

- A straight-forward and clear learning of BI, demonstrating its significance and relevance in professional environments.

- Understanding the key instruments and technologies that drive BI, covering the basics of data warehouses to the intricacies of predictive analytics.

- Hands-on comprehension of leveraging BI in situations ranging from streamlining operational tasks to improving customer interactions.

- Efficient methods for executing BI projects that assist you in identifying best practices and common pitfalls.

The realm of BI is continually changing, and this book aims to prepare managers, analysts, and entrepreneurs for the challenges and opportunities that await. Business Intelligence Essentials provides the skills and confidence needed to leverage data effectively and make better informed, impactful decisions.

Welcome to this journey of discovery, where you will learn and explore how data meets strategy to create powerful insights. Together, we will dive into the world of Business Intelligence and uncover its potential to transform the way you work, think, and make decisions. Let's get started!

How to use this book?

This book can be utilized in various ways, depending on your current level of BI knowledge and your specific goals:

1. **If you are new to BI:** Start with Chapter One and read through to the end. This will give you a strong understanding of the basics of BI. You can then dive into more advanced topics like data visualization, predictive analytics, and real-world applications.

2. **If you are familiar with basic BI concepts:** You could skip Chapter One and start with Chapter Two to understand how BI systems are built. From there, you can move on to Chapter Three, which provides an overview of popular BI tools. This Chapter will help you choose the right tool for your needs.

3. **If you are interested in data analytics techniques:** Chapters Four, Five, and Six will be particularly helpful in this case. Chapter Four focuses on Descriptive and Diagnostic Analytics. It teaches you how to analyze past data and understand why certain events occurred. Chapter Five covers Predictive Analytics and forecasting, enabling you to anticipate future trends. Chapter Six explores Prescriptive Analytics and Optimization. It provides techniques to identify the best course of action for achieving your goals.

4. **If your focus is on data visualization:** Chapter Seven will be your go-to resource. It covers the principles of effective data visualization and common chart types. It also sheds light on how to create compelling dashboards.

5. **For those interested in the practical aspects of BI implementation and management:** Chapters Eight, Nine and Ten provide insights on project management and change management. They also discuss user adoption

strategies and best practices for ensuring a successful BI implementation. You will also find here data governance and security techniques, and practical examples of successful BI implementations.

Who can benefit from this book?

Business Intelligence Essentials You Always Wanted to Know is an excellent resource for individuals seeking to enhance their understanding of Business Intelligence. It is ideal for applying BI concepts in today's data-driven business landscape. It offers insights on how to leverage BI for improved business performance, making it ideal for:

- Entrepreneurs and small business owners wanting to harness the power of data for growth

- Business analysts and data professionals looking to expand their skill set

- Managers and executives seeking to understand the strategic value of BI

- IT professionals involved in implementing or maintaining BI systems

- Market researchers, consultants, and anyone interested in understanding how data-driven decision-making can transform business operations

- Undergraduate and graduate students in business, information technology, and data science programs will find this book particularly useful as it provides a comprehensive overview of BI concepts, tools, and practical applications. The content is structured to build a strong foundation in BI, making it an excellent companion for academic courses.

This book combines theoretical concepts with practical applications, making it suitable for beginners entering the field of Business Intelligence. It also serves as a valuable guide for experienced professionals looking to stay updated on the latest trends and best practices.

This page is intentionally left blank

Chapter 1

Introduction to Business Intelligence

KEY LEARNING OBJECTIVES

- Define Business Intelligence and understand its core components.
- Explore the evolution and history of BI, from its early beginnings to modern advancements.
- Differentiate between Business Intelligence and Business Analytics.
- Recognize the importance and benefits of implementing BI in business operations.

In this chapter, you will be introduced to some of the foundational concepts and applications of Business Intelligence (BI). The purpose of this chapter is to lay the groundwork that we will build upon as we progress through the book.

1.1 What is Business Intelligence?

In today's fast-paced and data-driven world, the term "Business Intelligence" seems to be at the top of every company's agenda, and highlighted on everyone's CVs and LinkedIn profiles. But what does this term truly mean, and why has it become so indispensable?

Up to this point, "Business Intelligence" might have sounded like some fancy corporate buzzword, but it is actually a very practical concept. Picture yourself running a small trendy coffee shop. BI would be like having the accurate instinct for knowing when to brew extra lattes, which pastries would be best to stop selling, and what festive flavors will be popular this Christmas. Think of BI as a business's best ally, who always has the best advice.

In 1989, Howard Dresner, a well-known author and researcher, popularized the term "Business Intelligence," coming up with its accurate and popular definition: "concepts and methods to improve business decision-making by using fact-based support systems."[1]

In simpler terms, business intelligence is the mechanism that enables teams to make sense of data and guides them to informed decision-making. It encompasses a suite of processes and tools that empower businesses to transform raw data into meaningful information. Thus, one of the key benefits of implementing BI is that by using these tools, teams can better understand historical performance and leverage it to enhance future results.

Business intelligence helps us answer questions such as *"What happened earlier?"* and *"What is happening now?"* We will cover these questions in detail later in the book, along with the evolving scope of Business Intelligence. We will also explore the

---

1. Howard Dresner, *The Performance Management Revolution: Business Results Through Insight and Action*, (New York: John Wiley & Sons, 2007), 42.

interrelation between Business Intelligence and Business Analytics in the upcoming section.

1.1.1 Key components of business intelligence

Business intelligence may still sound like an abstract concept, but the picture starts getting much clearer when you understand the four key components that define business intelligence. These important elements are:

1. **Data collection:** The Business Intelligence process begins with gathering all your raw data including sales figures, customer feedback, social media metrics, etc.

2. **Data storage:** Next you would need a place to stash all this data, like a well-organized filing cabinet. This could be a fancy data warehouse or just a tidy spreadsheet.

3. **Data analysis:** This is where the real magic happens. As we progress through this vital step, we begin to uncover trends, patterns, and insights. If you are into board games as much as I am, you could think of it as a real-life game of "Clue," minus the drama. You are piecing together data to solve the mysteries of your business.

4. **Reporting/action:** Finally the big reveal, the moment we have been planning for. We could now happily share our findings. Depending on the use case and audience, this could be through a detailed report, a dashboard, or even a simple email update. The goal here is to make the data understandable and actionable.

To illustrate this, let's go back to a "real-world" example. We can change our barista role (from the early part of section 1.1) to something slightly different; we are now a Pilates instructor. Since we inaugurated our Pilates studio, we have been tracking attendance, class schedules, and social media engagement.

After only a few weeks, we started noticing that our evening classes were always packed, but the mornings were a bit of a hit or miss. After observing this, we decide to offer a special promotion for early birds. Well, there you have it; you have officially tapped into the power of BI. Figure 1.1 below is a visual representation of this example:

Figure 1.1   **A practical application of business intelligence**

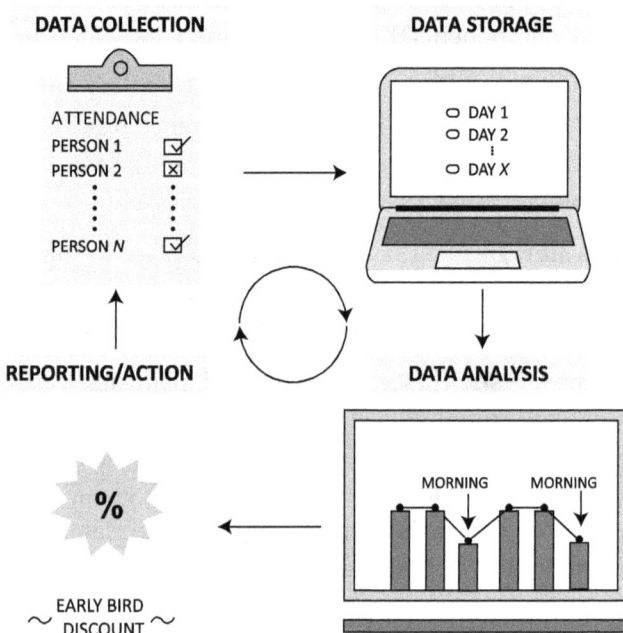

DATA COLLECTION

ATTENDANCE
PERSON 1 ☑
PERSON 2 ☒
⋮
PERSON *N* ☑

DATA STORAGE

○ DAY 1
○ DAY 2
⋮
○ DAY *X*

REPORTING/ACTION

%

EARLY BIRD
DISCOUNT

DATA ANALYSIS

MORNING   MORNING

Although this makes more sense now, you might still think, *"This sounds great, but how do I actually do all this?"* Don't worry, I am not exactly the patient type either. But as you go through this book, we will dig into all of the BI components in detail and cover practical tips and techniques. By the end of this book, you will not only understand the BI lingo—but also be ready to use it confidently in your own business and projects. Stick with me; we are just getting started!

1.2 Evolution and History of BI

Alright, get ready, because we are about to take a little stroll down memory lane. You might think business intelligence is this brand-new, modern concept, but the truth is, its beginnings go back quite a few decades. Ironically somehow, I find myself writing about history now, even though history was not exactly my favorite subject back in the day. However, I believe that understanding the origins of something can help us appreciate and grasp it a bit better. And I promise to keep it light!

1.2.1 The early days

The concept of business intelligence is not new—in fact, I can say with certainty that it is older than the two of us combined. It first popped up in the 19th century when Richard Millar Devens used the term in the book he published in 1865, *"Cyclopædia of Commercial and Business Anecdotes."*[2] Devens talked about Sir Henry Furnese, a merchant and politician, who started making smart business moves by gathering and acting upon key information before his competitors. This was BI in its earliest form, but it took another century before things really started to take off.[3]

1.2.2 The 1950s and 1960s: Arrival of computers

Fast-forward a few decades and we find businesses starting to use computers for basic data tasks. It might take some time to digest it, but those huge machines taking up entire rooms were already able to crunch numbers and store data fed through punch cards. Of course, data collection was manual and labor-intensive, but this era definitely set the stage for the data-driven processes we rely on today. It was not fancy, but looking back, it was the start of something big.

---

2. Richard Millar Devens, *Cyclopædia of Commercial and Business Anecdotes* (New York: D. Appleton and Company, 1865), 210.

3. Devens, *Appletons' Cyclopædia of Commercial and Business Anecdotes.*

1.2.3 The 1970s: Rise of Decision Support Systems

Of course, the advent of computers was only the first step. Soon after, a new ground-breaking technology came onto the scene and transformed the way we did business. You might not have heard this one before, but the star of this decade was the "Decision Support Systems (DSSs)." Quite a self-explanatory name; these systems were designed to help businesses make better decisions by providing them with interactive tools for data analysis.

Take a minute to process this—companies were no longer using computers to just store data, they were starting to harness that data to make informed decisions. DSSs brought structure and dynamism to the data world.

The term "DSSs" was first used by Scott Morton in the early 1970s, following his groundbreaking research at the Massachusetts Institute of Technology (MIT).[4] His work focused on the use of computer-based systems to assist in decision-making processes, particularly in complex business environments.

You might be wondering how DSSs actually work. To answer this, we can break them down into three main components:

1. **Database Management:** Handling data collection, storage, and retrieval.

2. **Model Management:** Providing tools and algorithms for data analysis, enabling simulations and what-if scenarios.

3. **User Interface:** Allowing non/less technical users to interact with the system, and generate reports and visualizations.

The implementation of DSS was truly an inflection point for BI. For the first time, people could ask specific questions through these systems (*i.e. how many customers could we attract with a 10% increase in our marketing budget?*) and receive immediate answers based on available data.

---

4. Scott Morton, *Management Decision Systems: Computer-Based Support for Decision Making* (Cambridge, MA: MIT Press, 1971), 35.

As you can imagine, this was a significant milestone and a shift from the static reports that businesses were used to consuming until then. If you are curious to learn more about successful early implementations of these systems, I would suggest researching Peter G. W. Keen and Charles Stabell's paper on the subject.[5]

It is not a surprise that DSS technology quickly became a vital tool for the strategizing and day-to-day operations of many businesses. Among others, manufacturing, finance, and logistics industries benefited from the implementation of DSSs and quickly began optimizing their forecasts and decision-making processes.

1.2.4 The 1980s: Relational databases

This era did not just revolutionize the music industry, it also brought a revolution into data management, with the introduction of relational databases. Companies like International Business Machines (IBM) Corporation changed how data was stored and accessed using Structured Query Language (SQL).

They brought data warehousing into the picture, providing companies with a way to consolidate vast amounts of data from multiple sources into one centralized place. As a result of this development, businesses started to get serious about organizing their data, and parallelly this opened the door to more advanced analyses and reporting.

1.2.5 The 1990s: Birth of modern BI

Even if the term had already been coined, it was not until this decade that the foundations of modern BI were laid and things truly started to take off. It was indeed during these years that businesses began to understand and embrace the power of their own data, going from just storing information to analyzing it.

Alongside this, companies like IBM, Oracle, and Microsoft also recognized fairly quickly the opportunity and market potential

---

5. Peter G. W. Keen and Charles Stabell, "Decision Support Systems: An Organizational Perspective," *Data Base 16*, no. 1 (Fall 1978): 3-15.

at stake and soon launched new BI tools that quickly became popular. One of the factors that helped these new tools gain popularity so rapidly was that now, users did not need to be technical professionals to be able to interact with them.

As more business users and households became familiar with computers, the technology industry continued to grow and saw more companies developing and selling their products and software. Of course, this simultaneously helped to bring prices down and engage even more users. In the evolution of BI, this period is usually referred to as "Business Intelligence 1.0."[6]

1.2.6 The 2000s: User-generated data and the boom of BI

Once we transitioned to the 21st century and realized we had survived the "year 2000 problem" (the Y2K problem)—the widespread concern about potential computers failing, due to the transition from the year 1999 to 2000—internet and mobile data became the main players in technology. We were introduced to Web 2.0, which compared to its older, read-only sibling, Web 1.0, enabled us to interact more with online content and also to generate it.

While we were all thriving—and some of us also embarrassing ourselves—with our blogger alter egos, little did we know back then that we were also becoming producers of data that would shape our online presence.

This shift to user-generated content represented a critical turning point. As more and more people started hopping on the internet bandwagon, social media platforms began to propagate, giving us new and fancier ways to fatten up the ever-growing pool of data.

I am sure you are making the connection already, but with these massive amounts of data being generated, companies had access to more information than ever before. They could get better insights into customer behavior and trends, which motivated them

---

6. "History of Business Intelligence," *CIO* (2018), retrieved from https://www.cio.com

to develop more advanced ways to utilize it. Rightly so, BI tools became more accessible and intuitive rapidly, reaching a broader audience.

The 2000s, known as Business Intelligence 2.0, also brought about the evolution of how we worked with data, with a powerful emphasis on data visualization. We no longer focused only on having our data structured and available, but we also cared to present it in a way that was easy to digest and act upon. This was when dashboards and visual analytics, which we'll explore more in Chapter Five, really started to shine.

1.2.7 The last decade (2010-2020): Big data and advanced analytics

In the latter half of this decade, big data and advanced analytics transformed BI with technologies like Hadoop and Spark. These tools unlocked the processing of massive datasets and the introduction of predictive and prescriptive analytics to the BI toolkit. We will dive deeper into these two concepts in Chapters Five and Six respectively.

During these recent years, another key factor that helped to democratize BI and made its processing and storage accessible to smaller businesses was the still highly relevant "Cloud Computing," which we will explore in the next chapter.

1.2.8 Today: Business Intelligence 3.0

It is fair to say, and potentially also what brought you to this book, that today BI has become an essential tool and practice in almost every industry. LinkedIn has since 2018 listed it as one of the top 25 skills most wanted by employers.[7]

We can now witness modern platforms offering real-time data analysis, smart data visualization, and powerful analytics features. Tools like Tableau, Power BI, and Qlik make it easy for businesses

---

7. LinkedIn Learning, "The Skills Companies Need Most in 2018—and the Courses to Get Them," retrieved from https://www.linkedin.com

to gain insights from their data, driving smarter decision-making and strategic planning. Today, these tools are a must in data-related job requirements.

Figure 1.2   **Timeline of business intelligence**

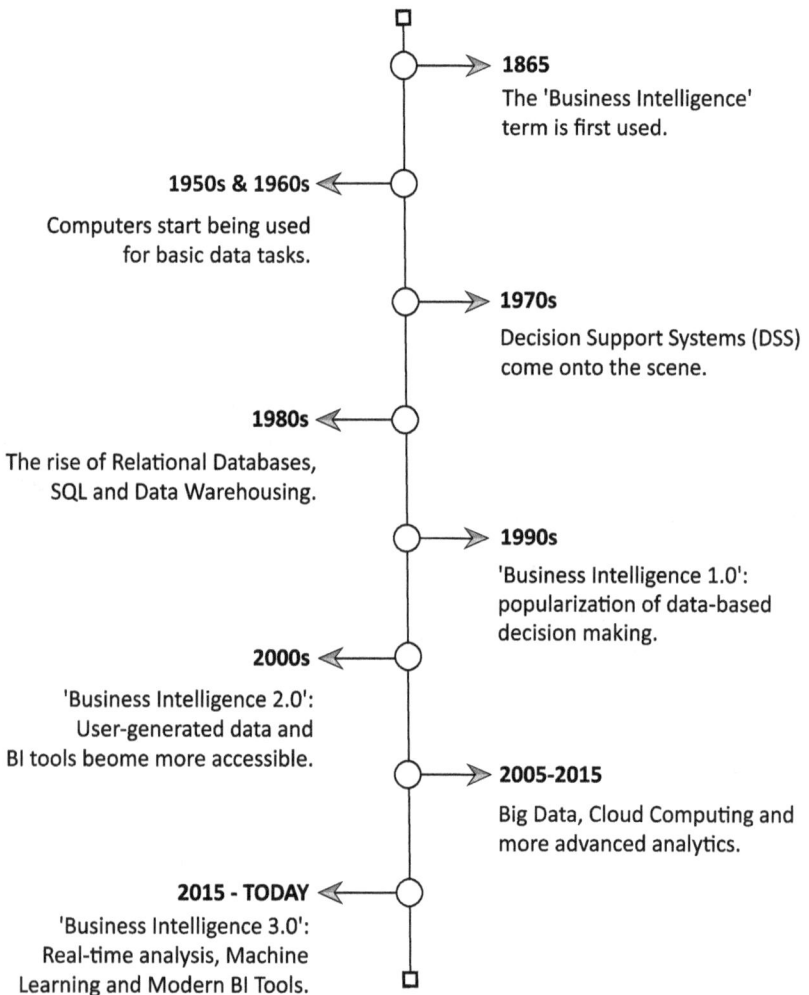

1865
The 'Business Intelligence' term is first used.

1950s & 1960s
Computers start being used for basic data tasks.

1970s
Decision Support Systems (DSS) come onto the scene.

1980s
The rise of Relational Databases, SQL and Data Warehousing.

1990s
'Business Intelligence 1.0': popularization of data-based decision making.

2000s
'Business Intelligence 2.0': User-generated data and BI tools beome more accessible.

2005-2015
Big Data, Cloud Computing and more advanced analytics.

2015 - TODAY
'Business Intelligence 3.0': Real-time analysis, Machine Learning and Modern BI Tools.

Wrapping up the history lesson

Here we are! You have successfully reached the end of this easy-to-follow journey through the evolution of business intelligence. If you are still with me, let's go through the comparison of two often confused terms: Business Intelligence (BI) and Business Analytics (BA).

1.3 Business Intelligence vs. Business Analytics

Since the origins and evolution of BI are now clear to us, it is a good moment to delve into a frequent debate topic in this field: the comparison between BI and BA. The truth is that a significant overlap exists between the two. However, there are also some key differences worth exploring.

1.3.1 Business intelligence: The wise advisor

Business intelligence is like looking in the rear-view mirror or having a wise advisor who learns from our previous experiences. Through BI, we can understand what happened in the past and why it happened. We can correctly answer questions like:

- How many units did we sell last quarter?
- Which product categories are performing best?
- What are our top customer demographics?

In short, business intelligence gives us a clear view of past and present business operations to support strategic decision-making.

1.3.2 Business analytics: The visionary

Meanwhile, business analytics is similar to peering into a crystal ball; it gives us a glimpse of what is coming. BA is more forward-looking, focusing on predicting future outcomes rather than just looking at data retrospectively. To achieve this, BA leverages more advanced techniques such as statistical models, algorithms, and machine learning, to accurately make predictions based on historical data. It's about answering questions like:

● What will our sales look like next quarter?

● Which products should we focus on to maximize profits?

● How can we optimize our supply chain?

BA dives deeper into the data, employing predictive analytics to forecast future trends and prescriptive analytics to suggest actions for achieving desired outcomes. It's not just about understanding what has happened, but also about figuring out what could happen and what should be done about it.

1.3.3 Key differences and overlaps

I am sure you are already identifying some variations and commonalities here, but let's break them down in more detail:

Table 1.1 **Comparison of business intelligence and business analytics**

Aspect	Business Intelligence	Business Analytics
Focus	Descriptive and diagnostic—focused on understanding past and present	Predictive and prescriptive—focused on forecasting future trends and suggesting actions
Tools	Dashboards, reports, and data visualization applications (i.e., Tableau, PowerBI)	More advanced techniques like statistics, machine learning algorithms, and predictive modeling
User Base	Frequently and widely used by non-technical business users and executives for strategic decision-making	Requires more technical knowledge, and therefore more often used by data scientists and analysts for in-depth analysis and forecasting
Output	Historical data-based insights, performance metrics and indicators, and trend analysis	Predictions, strategies for optimization, and recommendations on decisions for future activities

1.3.4 BI and BA: A dynamic duo

BI and BA are most powerful when used together. Think of BI as setting the foundation, by providing a clear understanding of the past and present, while BA builds on this foundation to predict and shape the future. For instance, consider a retailer seeking to gain a competitive edge. They might leverage business intelligence to thoroughly analyze past sales data and identify their most successful products historically.

Then they would turn to business analytics to take a more future-oriented approach—utilizing predictive models to forecast which emerging trends and items are more likely to be popular in the upcoming season. This would enable them to optimize their inventory and supply chain operations strategically to meet the anticipated consumer demand.

As technology advances, the lines between BI and BA become increasingly blurred. Therefore, it is relevant that we understand how they are connected and how they support each other. By doing so, we can navigate the full spectrum of analytic capabilities for business growth.

1.3.5 Practical example

Let's bring this to life with an example. Suppose you manage a chain of fitness centers. Using BI, you can analyze membership data to see which locations are performing best and identify trends in customer visits. Maybe you notice that attendance spikes in January, thanks to New Year's resolutions, but drops off in the summer.

With this BI insight, you can now apply BA to predict future membership trends and determine the best times to run promotions or add new classes. You might use predictive analytics to forecast that attendance will increase in the fall and prescriptive analytics to suggest offering a discounted membership rate to boost summer attendance.

1.3.6 Conclusion

In summary, while business intelligence and business analytics serve different purposes, they are both essential for a comprehensive understanding of your business. BI helps you learn from the past and understand the present, while BA helps you anticipate the future and make proactive decisions. By leveraging both, you can ensure that your business is not only reacting to current conditions but also strategically planning for what's ahead.

With this clear distinction in mind, you are now better equipped to harness the power of both BI and BA to drive your business forward. Next, we will explore the importance and benefits of BI in more detail.

1.4 Importance and Benefits of BI

I am certain you are already realizing how powerful and useful Business Intelligence can become, and you might already be thinking of scenarios where you could apply it. However, I still thought it would be beneficial to include this section in the First Chapter of the book. You may be finding your path at a start-up, leading your own business chain, or working at a multinational corporation; in all cases, BI can be a game-changer and I want you to have no doubt about this.

1.4.1 The value of business intelligence

In today's world where data is one of the most powerful assets a company can have, BI has become indispensable for any business aiming to stay competitive and efficient; and here is why:

1. **Informed decision-making:** One of BI's biggest appeals is how it enables businesses to make data-driven decisions. It helps you make decisions grounded in solid data, not just emerging from gut feelings, or based on some experienced

colleagues' assumptions. No more time and effort wasted reinventing the wheel. Instead, you take safe and meaningful steps.

2. **Improved efficiency:** BI tools help automate the mundane tasks of data collection and report generation, which we will understand in-depth later in the book. This enables businesses and teams to free up time to focus on analyzing and acting on the data, rather than just gathering it. It's like having an extra pair of hands that do all the heavy lifting for you.

3. **Competitive advantage:** While you try to stick out in these super-competitive, crowded markets, having timely, pertinent data at your fingertips can make all the difference. BI helps you identify market trends, customer preferences, and potential opportunities before your competitors do, giving you a significant edge.

4. **Refined customer insights:** While having timely data is crucial, it's also important to understand your clients and stay close to them. You want to ensure you are working towards creating and delivering what your customers want and are willing to pay for. This enables you to keep those loyal customers satisfied and coming back time and again. BI ensures this is possible by empowering you with detailed insights into customers' behavior, their preferences, and their buying habits.

5. **Cost saving:** Have you ever felt your company is leaking resources, but you can't identify where they are going? It is like the business has an unidentified hole in its pocket. This is where BI truly earns its keep. It is not magic, but it can certainly feel like it. BI digs through all the granular day-to-day data and finds where you are wasting time and cash, because only when you see it, you will be able to fix it. Spotting "waste" is a key part of lean thinking, and BI helps you apply it to your business's day-to-day operations.

6. **Increased revenue:** Essentially, all these benefits we just covered will result in more money in your pocket. Thus, the idea is that you should let BI guide your decisions, so that you can focus your efforts where they truly count.

1.4.2 Practical benefits of BI

Before finishing this chapter, I would like to illustrate the benefits of BI reviewed above with two practical examples:

Example 1: Travel agency

Imagine you run a travel agency. Following what we have covered so far in the book, you could use BI to analyze all the booking data from the trips you have sold since you launched your business two years ago, and spot trends and customer preferences. You may see that beach destinations are particularly popular during winter months, while adventure trips spike in the summer.

You could benefit from this finding by adjusting your advertising and social media campaigns accordingly, to ensure that you boost the right travel destinations at the right times. Since you also have numeric evidence from past months, you could discuss this data with hotels to get better deals ahead of the anticipated demand. Together, these findings will allow you to prepare your travel packages well in advance and have suitable offerings for your potential clients.

Example 2: Aesthetic clinic

For this other example, let's say you work at an aesthetic medicine clinic. After reading this book, you decide to implement BI and start analyzing patient data to look at two key areas; your most popular treatments and customer satisfaction. By looking at your treatment data, you discover that non-surgical procedures such as Botox are trending this year among a specific age group. At the same time, older patients prefer more intensive techniques such as laser treatment.

You take this data and findings to the commercial team and work together to adjust the treatments you offer and how you advertise them. In parallel, through the analysis you initiated on patients' feedback, you spot a couple of improvements that can be made to the appointment booking platform.

As we reach the end of this chapter, I hope you are convinced of the power of business intelligence and how it can be used to transform the way businesses operate.

Before moving into the next chapter, let's wrap up with a quick summary and a fun quiz to test your newfound knowledge.

Chapter Summary

◆ Business Intelligence (BI) is more than a corporate buzzword; it's a crucial tool for making well-informed business decisions.

◆ The importance of BI lies in its ability to transform raw data into actionable insights. This enables businesses to make smarter decisions, work more efficiently, understand customers better, cut costs, and increase revenue.

◆ BI has evolved significantly from its early days in the 1950s with basic data tasks, to the sophisticated tools we use today.

◆ The concept of Decision Support Systems (DSS) in the 1970s marked a major advancement in BI. This supported businesses to make better decisions through interactive data analysis.

◆ The 1980s saw the introduction of relational databases, revolutionizing data management and enabling more advanced analytics and reporting.

◆ The 1990s and 2000s brought about the rise of modern BI tools, making data analysis accessible to a broader audience and emphasizing data visualization.

◆ We distinguished between Business Intelligence and Business Analytics (BA), understanding that BI focuses on past and present data, while BA predicts future trends.

◆ BI and BA work best together, creating a comprehensive approach to understanding and optimizing business performance.

Quiz

1. **What is Business Intelligence (BI)?**
   a. A method to store large amounts of data
   b. A process for analyzing data and presenting actionable information
   c. A type of computer hardware
   d. A marketing strategy

2. **Which of the following is NOT a key component of Business Intelligence?**
   a. Data collection
   b. Data storage
   c. Application development
   d. Reporting

3. **Who first coined the term "*Business Intelligence*"?**
   a. Howard Dresner
   b. Richard Millar Devens
   c. Bill Gates
   d. Steve Jobs

4. **What decade saw the advent of Decision Support Systems (DSS)?**
   a. 1950s
   b. 1960s
   c. 1970s
   d. 1980s

5. **Which of these is an example of a data source in BI?**

   a. Sales database

   b. A physical filing cabinet

   c. A marketing strategy

   d. A conference room

6. **What is the main purpose of data storage in BI?**

   a. To delete unnecessary data

   b. To organize and keep data accessible

   c. To sell data to third parties

   d. To display data on a screen

7. **How does Business Intelligence help businesses?**

   a. By improving marketing strategies

   b. By transforming raw data into meaningful information

   c. By providing free data to all employees

   d. By eliminating the need for IT staff

8. **Which BI component is responsible for uncovering trends and insights?**

   a. Data collection

   b. Data storage

   c. Data analysis

   d. Reporting

9. **What technology revolutionized data management in the 1980s?**

   a. Relational databases

   b. Cloud computing

   c. Social media

   d. Blockchain

10. **What is Business Analytics (BA) focused on?**

    a. Historical data analysis

    b. Predicting future trends

    c. Data storage solutions

    d. IT infrastructure

Answers	1 – b	2 – c	3 – b	4 – c	5 – a
	6 – b	7 – b	8 – c	9 – a	10 – b

This page is intentionally left blank

Chapter **2**

BI Systems and Their Infrastructure

KEY LEARNING OBJECTIVES

- Explore the main components and architectures currently used to build BI systems.

- Understand data integration techniques leveraged in BI and when to best use each of them.

- Compare on-premise and cloud-based BI systems, and understand their respective advantages and challenges.

Welcome to Chapter Two. Now that we have covered the foundations of BI, we are going to get a bit more technical (I will still aim to keep it light, I promise) and learn about how BI systems are built, what they are composed of, and the different structures available.

2.1 Key Components of BI Systems

We briefly introduced this topic at the beginning of Chapter One, and now it is time to expand on it. To make this slightly more interesting, let's use an analogy to cover this section.

Following the hype they have been getting during the last couple of years, I decided we could compare the composition of a BI system with that of a campervan. Let's begin!

Figure 2.1	An illustration of the key components of a BI system

2.1.1 Data sources

Just as we would line up all the individual parts for our dream campervan (engine, tires, metal sheets), data sources are also our raw materials. These vary depending on the industry or team that we operate in, but some standard examples are: sales databases, spreadsheets, Customer Relationship Management (CRM) systems, and social media interactions. The more diverse and richer our raw materials, the better quality our final outcome (campervan vs insights) will be.

2.1.2 Data integration

With our raw materials at hand, we can begin assembling all the functional elements. For our comfy camper, this may be the chassis, which is the load-bearing framework of the vehicle. In BI this would often represent converting our data into working formats and storing it in a central repository. Just as we would put together the wiring and plumbing of our mobile home, this step ensures all our data is stored in the right place and in a usable configuration.

Before BI tools proliferated, data from all the different sources would be isolated and stored in separate locations. The emergence of this technology enabled their combined storage so that more advanced analytics and tooling could process the data at a later stage.

Find below the key approaches to execute data integration:

Table 2.1 **Overview of data integration technologies**

Type	Tools	Definition	When to Use
Extract, Transform, Load (ETL)	Talend, Apache Nifi, Microsoft SSIS	The most traditional and widely used technique; consists of 3 steps: Extract data from data sources (E), Transform or convert it into a suitable format (T), and load it into the central repository (L)	Ideal when data needs to be processed with a specific frequency (i.e., daily, weekly)
Extract, Load, Transform (ELT)	Amazon Redshift, Google BigQuery, Snowflake	An alteration of ETL that leverages the processing power of more modern data warehousing solutions	Suitable for those cases where data has to be stored quickly, and can be transformed later for specific analyses
Change Data Capture (CDC)	Oracle GoldenGate, Microsoft SQL Server CDC, Talend	Its focus is to identify and capture only data that has changed since the last update (incremental); this approach minimizes the amount of data to be processed.	Great for real-time data and scenarios where data freshness is critical

Type	Tools	Definition	When to Use
Application Programming Interface (API)	MuleSoft, Zapier, Microsoft Power Automate	This approach enables communication and data exchange between different software applications, without manual data movement.	Recommended when businesses need to connect disparate systems
Data Virtualization	Denodo, Cisco Data Virtualization, IBM Data Virtualization Manager	Allows access and queries to data from multiple sources without physically moving it; which is achieved by creating a virtual layer. This approach avoids data duplication.	Ideal for real-time data integration, and cases where quick access is preferred

2.1.3 Data warehousing

We are making good progress here. We have all our components ready, and we would probably now proceed with their installation into the vehicle's structure; exactly as we would do with our data warehouse. Interestingly, both the data warehouse and the camper's cabinets would perform a very similar function here: organizing all our stuff into compartments, ensuring it is accessible and ready to be used.

Several Data Warehousing Architectures have been developing and gaining popularity over the past few decades. Find a detailed explanation in Table 2.2 below:

Table 2.2	Overview of data warehousing architectures		
Architecture	**Origin**	**Definition**	**When to Use**
Traditional Data Warehouse	1980s	An old, reliable classic; this approach uses Extract, Transform, Load (ETL) processes to gather data from multiple sources into a centralized repository. The data is analyzed in-depth using Online Analytical Processing (OLAP) tools. The resulting insights can then be presented through interactive dashboards and detailed reports.	Best suited for managing large volumes of structured data, and conducting in-depth historical analysis
Data Lake	2010	This setup stores raw data in its original format until it is needed, offering flexibility and the capacity to handle vast amounts of data. Popular tools for developing data lakes are Microsoft Azure and Amazon S3.	Useful with large volumes of unstructured and semi-structured data. Optimal for big data uses and advanced analytics
Modern Data	The early 2010s	Combination of the two architectures mentioned above, and uses both ETL and Extract, Load, Transform (ELT) processes to work with data. Known examples are Google BigQuery and Azure Synapse.	Large volumes of structured and unstructured data

Architecture	Origin	Definition	When to Use
Cloud-Based BI	Late 2000s	Configuration that leverages cloud computing and offers scalability, flexibility, and affordable prices. Popular alternatives are AWS, Azure, and Google Cloud.	Real-time data and advanced analytics
Federated BI	The early 2010s	This structure stores data in its original source systems, and BI tools can access and interact with this data directly from there. This reduces duplication and enables real-time access. It can add complexity but compensates by granting higher flexibility.	Real-time data and advanced analytics

As seen in Table 2.2 above, diverse data warehousing architectures serve different purposes, and choosing the right data warehousing environment for your BI system is a crucial step. Considering the significance of data warehousing in BI, I would like us to delve into this topic further, later in the chapter.

2.1.4 Data modeling

We now have a functioning campervan structure, and we probably want to pay close attention to the design of our internal layout, ensuring everything fits and follows an effective blueprint, pretty much as we would do with data modeling.

This step would be like creating a visual representation of data mapping; showing how all our data is connected and organized. This is why this part of the process is crucial, both for building our camper and structuring our data. It ensures that we design an accurate layout that makes everything easy to locate and to use later on.

Find below a simple representation of what the output of this step looks like:

Figure 2.2   **An illustration of data modeling**

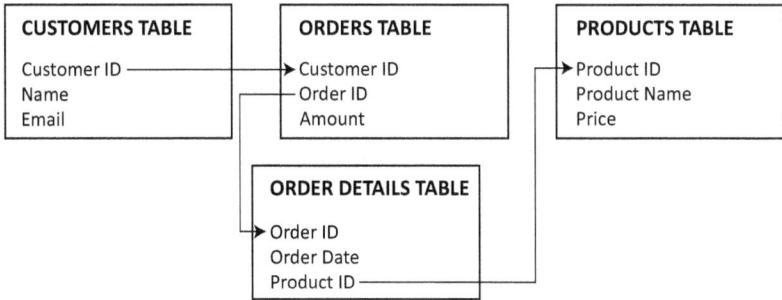

CUSTOMERS TABLE	ORDERS TABLE	PRODUCTS TABLE
Customer ID	Customer ID	Product ID
Name	Order ID	Product Name
Email	Amount	Price

ORDER DETAILS TABLE

Order ID
Order Date
Product ID

2.1.5 Online Analytical Processing (OLAP) tools

This is looking good, you might want to start deciding your road trip destination! With the frame and interiors in place, I would suggest bringing some diagnostic tools to check everything is working as expected (i.e., sensors, suspension). Similarly, OLAP tools, such as Oracle OLAP and Microsoft Analysis Services, through calculations and trend analyses, can validate that our data interactions are smooth and efficient.

2.1.6 BI reporting and visualization tools

The last part of this puzzle - time to get into the interactive side of things. In the case of our mobile home, the dashboard and control panel will show key information for us to be able to drive safely. Likewise, BI reporting and visualization tools such as Tableau, Power BI, and Qlik will empower us to fairly and intuitively build reports and dashboards, turning raw data into insights that are easy to digest. We will dive deeper into BI tools in Chapter Three.

2.1.7 Conclusion

I appreciate this might have been quite a tedious section, even if I tried to put a bit of a lighter spin on it with the campervan analogy. However, I believe it is important for you to have a notion of the key elements of BI systems, as this way you will be better equipped to:

1. Participate in the design of the BI configuration that is just right for your business.

2. Unlock the full potential of your data.

2.2 Data warehousing: On-Premise vs. Cloud-Based BI systems

As anticipated when covering the key components of BI in section 2.1, choosing the right data warehousing solution will be one of the first major decisions you will need to make when setting up your BI system. Each data warehousing alternative has its pros and cons, and the right choice for your business will depend on various factors such as security requirements, available budget, etc. Let's go ahead and get familiar with both data warehousing options:

- **On-Premises:** Commonly known as "on-prem," it requires the installation of BI software on physical local servers and infrastructure and is therefore privately owned and controlled by the organization. This traditional approach gives you full control over your data, systems, and their configuration. However, the initial disbursement required for this option would be much higher.

  This is a good time to introduce the concept of "database scalability," which refers to the ability of a database to handle increasing amounts of data and users, without decreasing its performance. On-premises BI systems are often unable to scale databases in this way, making scalability a known challenge for on-prem solutions and a big advantage of choosing cloud data warehousing systems.

- **Cloud-Based:** Here system resources are hosted and delivered over the internet or "the cloud." Therefore, they are not physically owned nor personally managed but accessible from anywhere with an internet connection. Third-party service providers are responsible for the maintenance and updates of cloud-based systems. They also facilitate most of the security configuration and compliance of these systems.

  Cloud-based BI systems operate on a pay-as-you-go pricing model, where businesses only pay for the resources they utilize. This flexible model means businesses can easily decide when to increase hired storage and computing power to adjust their scalability.

While we are on the subject, it is important to note that the advent of cloud technology has played a crucial role in the development of Artificial Intelligence (AI). We will delve deeper into this topic in Chapter 10.

Cloud services such as Amazon Web Services (AWS), Google Cloud Platform (GCP), and Microsoft Azure have made it possible to access the massive computational power and storage needed to handle and analyze large datasets. This has been fundamental for training complex AI models. Without the scalable and flexible infrastructure offered by cloud technology, many of the AI applications we see today would have been challenging to implement.

2.2.1 Making the choice

As mentioned earlier, the decision of which alternative to move forward with, will depend on multiple factors unique to each person/business use case. However, let's make this decision easier by breaking down the key considerations in a more digestible format. In the table/cheat sheet below, I have summarized the main points to assess so that you are better equipped to choose the best fit for your needs.

Table 2.3   **Summary of the key data warehousing characteristics**

Aspect	On-Premises	Cloud
Control	Full, over hardware and software	Limited, managed by the service provider
Customization	High	Limited
Performance	Potentially higher, as the system is localized	Tied to an internet connection
Security	Higher control	Mostly managed by the service provider
Cost	High for initial setup, lower recurring costs	Low for initial setup, pay-as-you-go model afterwards
Maintenance	In-house Information Technology (IT) team	Managed by the service provider
Scalability	Challenging and costly	Simple and very flexible

Before closing up this topic, let me share with you some real examples of businesses that have successfully used each of these systems:

Table 2.4	Real examples of data warehousing implementation

On-Premises		
Coca-Cola	**Toyota**	**Bank of America**
To manage its vast amounts of data from sales, distribution, and logistics	To analyze large datasets related to manufacturing, supply chain management, and quality control	To ensure sensitive financial data remains secure and complies with stringent regulatory requirements
Cloud		
Netflix *(via AWS)*	**Airbnb** *(via AWS)*	**Spotify** *(via GCP)*
To handle vast amounts of data generated from user interactions and streaming habits	To analyze data from millions of listings, guest interactions, and booking transactions	To perform large-scale analytics, that deliver personalized music recommendations, and improve user engagement

Chapter Summary

◆ Understanding the fundamental components of BI systems, such as data sources, data integration techniques, and data warehousing, and how they're essential for building a robust BI infrastructure.

◆ Data integration techniques like ETL, ELT, CDC, API integration, and data virtualization each have unique benefits and ideal use cases, enabling effective data management and analysis.

◆ Various data warehousing architectures, including Traditional Data Warehouses, Data Lakes, Modern Data Warehouses, Cloud-Based BI, and Federated BI, offer different advantages depending on the organization's needs and the nature of the data.

◆ The choice between on-premise and cloud-based BI systems depends on several factors, including control, customization, performance, security, cost, maintenance, and scalability.

Quiz

1. **What is the main function of data sources in a BI system?**

   a. Store the final reports

   b. Provide raw data for analysis

   c. Visualize the data

   d. Secure the data

2. **Which BI system component is responsible for gathering raw data from various sources?**

   a. Data storage

   b. Data collection

   c. Data analysis

   d. Reporting

3. **In the context of BI, what does ETL stand for?**

   a. Extract, Transform, Load

   b. Execute, Transfer, Load

   c. Extract, Transfer, Load

   d. Execute, Transform, Load

4. **Which tool is commonly used for Extract, Transform, and Load (ETL) processes?**

   a. Tableau

   b. Talend

   c. Power BI

   d. Qlik

5. **Which data integration technique is known for identifying and capturing only the data that has changed since the last update?**

   a. ETL

   b. ELT

   c. CDC

   d. Data virtualization

6. **What does API stand for in the context of data integration?**

   a. Application Programming Interface

   b. Automated Process Integration

   c. Advanced Programming Interface

   d. Application Process Integration

7. **Which data integration technique is ideal for real-time data integration and quick access without data duplication?**

   a. ETL

   b. ELT

   c. CDC

   d. Data virtualization

8. **What is the purpose of data modeling in BI?**

   a. To store raw data

   b. To create visual representations of data mappings

   c. To execute complex algorithms

   d. To clean and preprocess data

9. **What is a key benefit of using a data warehouse in BI?**

   a. Reduces the need for data analysis

   b. Centralizes data from multiple sources

   c. Eliminates the need for data visualization

   d. Increases manual data entry

10. **Which architecture stores raw data in its original format until it is needed?**

    a. Traditional data warehouse

    b. Data lake

    c. Modern data warehouse

    d. Federated BI

Answers	1 – b	2 – b	3 – a	4 – b	5 – c
	6 – a	7 – d	8 – b	9 – b	10 – b

This page is intentionally left blank

Chapter **3**

BI Tools and Technologies

KEY LEARNING OBJECTIVES

- Get familiar with some popular BI tools and their features.
- Understand how to assess and choose the right BI tool for your needs.

Now that we have covered the foundational knowledge of BI, if you are still here with me, you might be feeling slightly overwhelmed by all these new concepts, and wondering how to actually go about implementing them. If that is the case, this chapter is for you.

We are about to get a lot more practical here. The goal is that after reading this chapter, you will already be able to start implementing BI in your own environment. From this point on, we will work together to build on the BI skills and knowledge you are gaining, as you progress through the rest of the book.

3.1 Overview of Popular BI Tools

Before getting started, I would like to clarify that the ranking of BI tools I am about to share in this section is one I have curated myself, based on my own research and personal experiences.

Depending on who you ask or what sources you use for your research, this ranking will vary.

When you think about it, it makes sense that there isn't a single official ranking. After all, different teams and businesses have their own needs, and what might be suitable for one could be completely unsuitable for another organization with different requirements. That said, find below an overview of the most widely known BI tools:

1. Power BI

(https://www.microsoft.com/en-us/power-platform/products/power-bi); from $10 per user and month; free tier available

Power BI, brought to you by Microsoft, integrates seamlessly with other Microsoft products. This makes it a go-to for businesses and teams already using the Microsoft ecosystem. It is powerful, yet easy to use, and perfect for all sorts of data analytics needs.

It is usually very popular with people wanting to get started with data analysis, that's why I am adding it here at the top of my ranking. There's a free desktop version that often covers the needs of individuals or smaller projects, but publishing reports online and using certain collaboration features typically requires the paid license. It offers a cloud-based deployment; however, it has been reported to slow down when handling large datasets or sharing reports online.

Notable features of this tool are:

- Real-time data access
- Customizable dashboards
- AI-driven insights
- Integration with Excel and other Microsoft tools

2. Tableau

(https://www.tableau.com/products/desktop); from $15 per user and month

Tableau, part of the Salesforce family, is like the Swiss Army knife of BI tools. It is incredibly versatile, with a user-friendly interface that allows you to create stunning visualizations and interactive dashboards with just a few clicks.

It can be deployed both on cloud and on-premises infrastructure and stands out for its geospatial data processing and visualization capabilities. However, users frequently say that learning how to use the more powerful functions of Tableau can be difficult without training.

Some of its key features are:

- Drag-and-drop interface
- Extensive data connectivity options
- Real-time analytics
- Collaboration tools

3. Qlik Sense

(https://www.qlik.com/us/products/qlik-sense); from $30/month, quote-based

This tool is ideal for medium and large organizations that need to perform complex data analysis and create highly interactive visualizations, thanks to its powerful engine and fast processing performance for large queries and analyses.

Qlik Sense, with both on-prem and cloud-based deployment, is known to be particularly useful for uncovering insights that may not be immediately obvious. However, it is often reported that its more powerful features and customization involve a steep learning process that, quite frequently, is hard to overcome due to the lack of good training material.

A few core capabilities are:

- Powerful engine and data models
- In-memory processing
- Interactive dashboards
- Advanced analytics

4. Looker

(https://cloud.google.com/looker); ~$2900/month, quote-based

Now part of Google Cloud, and deployed both through the cloud and on-prem, Looker offers a modern BI platform with strong data modeling capabilities and integration with Google's cloud ecosystem. Its pricing makes it more restrictive and more suitable for medium/large enterprises, but I decided to keep it in this ranking due to its popularity. You will likely hear about this tool as you get more familiar with BI systems.

Some of its main features:

- Access to real-time data
- Local database
- Embedded analytics into other applications
- Built-in collaboration tools

5. Sisense

(https://www.sisense.com/); ~$1500/month

A well-known business intelligence and data analytics platform designed to simplify complex data analysis into easily digestible charts and maps. The pricing of this tool might not make it suitable for smaller teams, although it could be a good option for teams with a more generous budget, as its package also includes high-quality customer service.

As was the case for Qlik Sense, some of Sisense's more advanced analytics can only be leveraged by users with more technical knowledge. Less experienced users might find it challenging to use the tool initially.

Key functionalities are:

- Drill-down functionality
- Action-driven analytics
- High level of customization
- Real-time collaboration

Other business intelligence software you might have heard of, or will get to know as you gain more experience in this field, are: Oracle BI, SAP Business Objects, SAS Visual Analytics, Zoho Analytics, and Domo.

Given that you now have a sense of the leading BI tools available, I suggest going a step further and checking with your colleagues if you can get access to the ones already available in your company. You may also give the free trials a go on your own to see which one works better for your use case and personal preferences.

Of course, there is no harm in getting familiar with one or more tools, either learning on your own or on the job. If you are someone looking for either a new job or a career change currently, you can boost your CV by learning and listing the most common BI tools in the "skills" section. Hiring managers often look for candidates with experience in specific BI tools.

3.2 How to Choose a BI Tool

I get it; with all the alternatives we have just covered, you may encounter a situation of "analysis paralysis." We have all been there. With so many options available, it can be overwhelming to decide where to start, unless your company has already made this decision for you. In any case, let me help you with the following guide to navigate this selection process.

1. **Understand your needs**

   Before you start shopping around, I suggest you take some time to assess your current requirements. A few items you could consider are:

   - How much data are you working with?

   - How complex is your data; is it structured/ semi-structured/unstructured?

   - Who are going to be the main users of the tool? How technically-aware are they?

   - What are the must-have features? Does the tool need to offer real-time data processing? Do you want to be able to customize your visualizations?

2. **Budget considerations**

   As covered in the previous section 3.1, BI tools come in all shapes and sizes, and so do their price tags. Some are free, some subscription-based, and others come with a substantial license price. Thus, it is crucial to first assess your needs as seen above and find the right balance with what you can afford.

3. **Integration capabilities**

   Your BI tool needs to be well synchronized with other tools and systems at your workplace. This is why I would also recommend checking how easily it can integrate with your applications and data sources. Can the tool gather and consolidate data from your various sources? How easy is it to connect the BI tool to the other applications you and your team frequently use? These parameters might not seem like a lot, but they will hugely optimize the adoption stage and ensure a smooth collaboration.

4. Ease of use

No matter how powerful the BI tool is, it won't be very helpful if it is too complicated for your team to use. Especially when getting started and introducing this technology to your teams/peers for the first time, I highly recommend starting with tools with an intuitive user interface (UI), that both technical and non/less technical folks can access and enjoy. Additionally, I would suggest checking the available training materials that the tool provider or even industry experts might offer, as well as the level of customer support.

Choosing your first business intelligence tool is a big decision, but I assure you that carefully assessing your alternatives will pay off in the long run.

Chapter Summary

◆ Overview of popular BI tools, including Power BI, Tableau, Qlik Sense, Looker, and Sisense, with their key features and suitability for different business needs.

◆ Key considerations for choosing a BI tool include: understanding your needs, budget constraints, integration capabilities, and ease of use.

◆ It is essential to evaluate BI tools based on user requirements, data complexity, and available resources to ensure the chosen tool aligns with business goals and promotes efficient decision-making processes.

Quiz

1. **What should you assess before choosing a BI tool?**
   a. Current data and complexity
   b. Historical performance of the tool
   c. Competitors' tools
   d. All of the above

2. **Which feature is crucial for ensuring a BI tool's integration capabilities?**
   a. Customer support
   b. Data visualization options
   c. Ability to connect to various data sources
   d. Cost-effectiveness

3. **What aspect should be considered regarding the ease of use of a BI tool?**
   a. Number of features
   b. User interface design
   c. Cost
   d. Integration capabilities

4. **Why is it beneficial to get familiar with more than one BI tool?**
   a. To increase costs
   b. To improve decision-making
   c. To reduce data complexity
   d. To decrease data integration

5. **What should you consider about the budget when choosing a BI tool?**

   a. Only the initial cost

   b. Only the subscription cost

   c. Both initial and ongoing costs

   d. The cost is irrelevant

6. **What is a critical factor for the success of a BI tool in an organization?**

   a. The number of users

   b. The complexity of the interface

   c. The alignment with business goals

   d. The cost of the tool

7. **What is the first step in choosing a BI tool?**

   a. Evaluating the cost

   b. Assessing your current needs

   c. Checking the tool's reviews

   d. Asking colleagues

8. **What is the main purpose of identifying key metrics before choosing a BI tool?**

   a. To ensure data security

   b. To align with business objectives

   c. To determine the cost

   d. To simplify the interface

9. **Which tool is recommended for users already in the Microsoft ecosystem?**
    a. Tableau
    b. Looker
    c. Power BI
    d. Qlik Sense

10. **Which BI tool is ideal for medium and large organizations needing complex data analysis?**
    a. Power BI
    b. Sisense
    c. Qlik Sense
    d. Oracle BI

Answers	1 – a	2 – c	3 – b	4 – b	5 – c
	6 – c	7 – b	8 – b	9 – c	10 – c

This page is intentionally left blank

Chapter 4

Descriptive and Diagnostic Analytics

KEY LEARNING OBJECTIVES

- Understand the fundamentals of descriptive analytics and its role in BI.
- Understand the fundamentals of diagnostic analytics, and how it complements descriptive analytics.
- Gain skills in creating and interpreting business intelligence reports.
- Explore real-world case studies to see descriptive and diagnostic analytics in action.

Since we are now hands-on with BI tools and technologies, why not delve into the heart of business intelligence? This chapter is all about making sense of your data's past and present trends and understanding the underlying reasons behind those trends. By the end of this chapter, you will also have a much more extensive knowledge of how BI reports work and how they are developed.

4.1 Introduction to Descriptive Analytics

Borrowing Gartner's[8] definition, we can explain Descriptive Analytics as "the examination of data or content, usually manually performed, to answer the question *'what happened?'* or *'what is happening?'* characterized by traditional business intelligence and visualizations." Therefore, the process of descriptive analytics helps us understand past and present events, as well as identify relevant trends and anomalies. It enables us to make better-informed decisions for the future.

4.1.1 Implementation

Our example in Chapter One about the Pilates instructor is a great illustration of how descriptive analytics works within a business intelligence framework. We already saw how by tracking attendance, class schedules, and social media engagement, the instructor was able to identify trends and make informed decisions to improve their business performance. In this case, the decision was to implement the "Early Bird promotion" to boost attendance during morning sessions.

Now, let's break this example down to see what the process of applying descriptive analytics within a BI context would look like:

1. **Identifying KPIs**

    To execute descriptive analytics in BI, we not only need to have access to historical data, but we should also define a set of metrics to measure our business performance; these are frequently known as Key Performance Indicators (KPIs). Putting our pilates instructor hat back on, some KPIs we would likely monitor are: class attendance rates, customer retention rates (how often clients come back for more classes), and booking cancellation rates. For this first step, the metrics we define must be chosen carefully so that they

---

8. Gartner, "Descriptive Analytics," retrieved from https://www.gartner.com

reflect our primary business goals and enable effective BI practices.

2. **Collecting data**

Now that we have identified our relevant metrics, the next step in the BI process consists of finding the right data and data sources that will allow us to update those metrics. These could vary depending on the business and the data collection processes. Some examples of data sources are: spreadsheets, databases in a data warehouse, social media websites, etc. In our case, we would leverage the spreadsheets where we track the classes delivered, the schedule of classes and attendance, and the database where we store registration details from each customer.

3. **Preparing data**

Even if this is a relatively simple example, we can observe that there are already different types of data sources such as spreadsheets and databases. Thus, for our next step, we will work on merging these different datasets, so that we can connect them and analyze them jointly. Again, this is a vital step of data analysis in business intelligence, as only with this step we can bring all the pieces of the puzzle together and see the whole picture.

For our pilates example, we will combine the attendance data from the spreadsheets with the customer information from our database. To keep it simple, we could extract/download the data from the database, and bring it into the spreadsheet where we track the schedule and attendance. Once both datasets are merged, we will be able to start seeing connections and trends that would not be apparent if we looked at the data separately. For instance, we may identify that the highest cancellation rates come from a specific age group. See below Figure 4.1 for a visual illustration.

| Figure 4.1 | **A practical application of data preparation** |

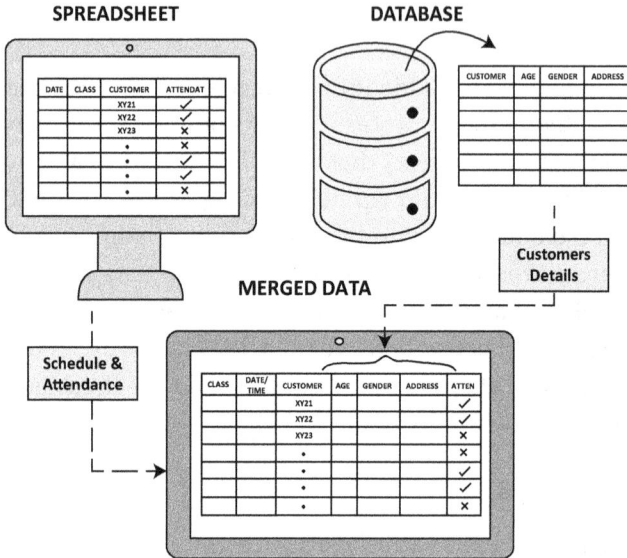

4. Analyzing data

With our data ready, it is time to start analyzing it. Data analysis in the business intelligence framework could be a book or a couple on its own, but allow me to summarize it here for you. By performing data analysis, we will be able to interpret our data and extract meaningful conclusions and insights. Of course, there are countless ways of analyzing data; some are manual such as calculations on spreadsheets, and others are mostly automated through tools like Power BI.

Let's assume our pilates instructor is just getting started in this field. I would then suggest sticking to the software already being used to handle the spreadsheets, which is Microsoft Excel. They could group customers into age ranges, and calculate their average attendance and cancellation ratios. The instructor could also build some simple visualizations like bar charts and line graphs to show key metrics at a glance (see Fig. 4.2), such as attendance trends over the past month and the most popular class times.

Figure 4.2 **Example of data visualization**

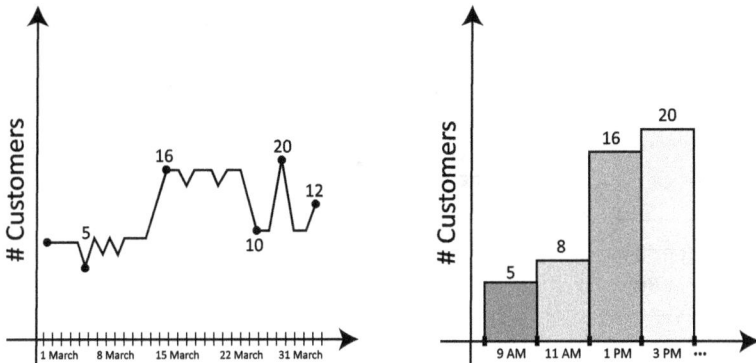

5. **Presenting data**

Finally, for the last step in our BI process for descriptive analytics, we can leverage the data visualizations and analysis we built in the previous step, and craft an easy-to-digest report. We could then share this report with our leadership team to inform them of the current progress, and present suggestions for the next steps. Our pilates instructor might want to create a dashboard in Excel that shows the key metrics at a glance, such as the attendance over a specific period, which they can then easily update and monitor.

By following these five steps, our instructor would have built a new BI system for their business using descriptive analytics. This allows them to observe patterns and trends as the studio grows and take quick and timely actions when KPIs fall behind expectations.

A visual representation of this process is shown below in Figure 4.3:

Figure 4.3 **Summary of the descriptive analytics process**

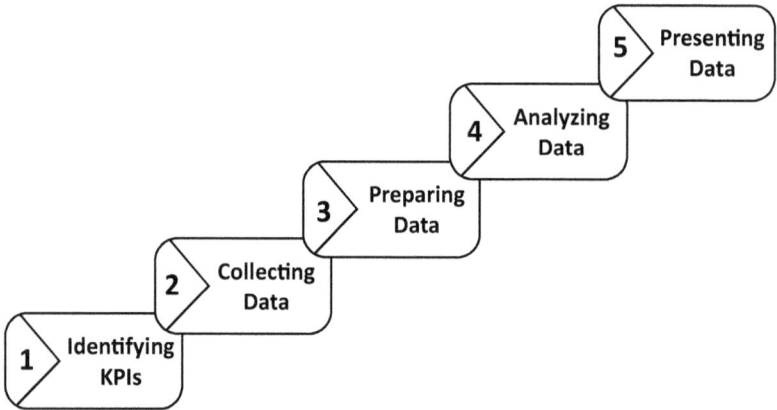

4.1.2 Benefits of descriptive analytics

Understanding *"what happened"* through descriptive analytics in BI provides several benefits:

- **Improved decision-making:** By understanding past performance, we are equipped to make smarter decisions moving forward.

- **Effective reporting:** With a clear view of our historical performance, we can also leverage this BI framework to improve how insights are communicated and shared across our teams; simplifying complex data into digestible visualizations and reports.

- **Enhanced operational efficiency:** As we uncover trends and patterns, we can also compare and benchmark them with historical data and set realistic goals.

- **Better customer insights:** Identifying our customers' behaviors and preferences will enable us to tailor our strategies to meet their needs and expectations, in turn driving more sales and profitability.

- **Resource allocation:** By learning our areas of success and inefficiency, we will be more prepared to correctly prioritize efforts and investments, and better manage our resources.

4.1.3 Disadvantages of descriptive analytics

The disadvantages of focusing exclusively on descriptive analytics are as follows:

- Limited predictive power, as this analysis focuses mainly on past data

- Surface-level insights, without diving deep into underlying causes behind the observed patterns

- Potential for misinterpretation; data could be misunderstood or misinterpreted without having the adequate context/ background

- High dependence on historical data, which could skew BI results if this past data is either inaccurate or incomplete

To sum up, descriptive analytics in BI is like having a printed itinerary of where our business has been. It will not help us to predict future performance, but it provides a strong base we can build on with the techniques we will continue covering in the upcoming sections.

4.2 Introduction to Diagnostic Analytics

Leveraging Gartner's glossary[9] again, Diagnostic Analytics is defined as the "form of advanced analytics that examines data or content to answer the question, *'Why did it happen?'* This form of analysis is an integral part of the BI process, and it is characterized by techniques such as drill-down, data discovery, data mining, and correlations."

4.2.1 Implementation

Through descriptive analytics, we understood "what had happened" with the lower attendance in morning pilates sessions. As a logical next step, diagnostic analytics in BI will enable us to comprehend *"why"* this could be happening. This step can be implemented manually or with the support of statistical software such as Microsoft Excel, Tableau, and R.

Regardless of how you decide to proceed, first it is important to understand some of the diagnostic analytics techniques used most frequently within the business intelligence framework:

1. **Hypothesis Testing**

   Through this statistical technique, we will create a hypothesis and test it against the evidence and data we have collected, enabling us to prove or disprove our educated guess.

   To create a hypothesis for diagnostic analytics, we will define a historically oriented statement. In our example, this statement could be: *"The opening of a new fitness studio has caused a decline in morning class attendance at our Pilates studio."* This will direct our analysis and remind us of what we are testing.

   Now, to test the hypothesis, we could use our data from the morning classes and we could also gather data on the

---

9. Gartner, "Diagnostic Analytics," retrieved from https://www.gartner.com

other studio's class schedule. If the analysis were to show a significant drop in attendance coinciding with the opening of that other studio, our hypothesis would be supported. With the initial assumption now tested and proved, we could work on defining a set of actions to address this, like amending our schedule, investing in marketing strategies, etc.

2. **Root Cause Analysis (RCA)**

   This technique in the BI process will help us to understand the root causes or underlying reasons of a problem, rather than just its symptoms. By establishing clear causation, we will be able to accurately identify the right solutions to address the source of the problem and prevent it from happening again.

Let's suppose our pilates studio owner has noticed a significant drop in customer retention rates and wants to get to the bottom of this. First, we would need to define the problem, "the decline in customer retention rates," and gather relevant data such as attendance register, class schedules, and customer feedback. For this analysis, we could leverage a very popular and simple technique for identifying root causes, the "5 Whys," where we keep asking ourselves *why* until we uncover the fundamental issue causing the problem. Find below an illustration of what this could look like:

| Figure 4.4 | **Example of a 5-Why analysis** |

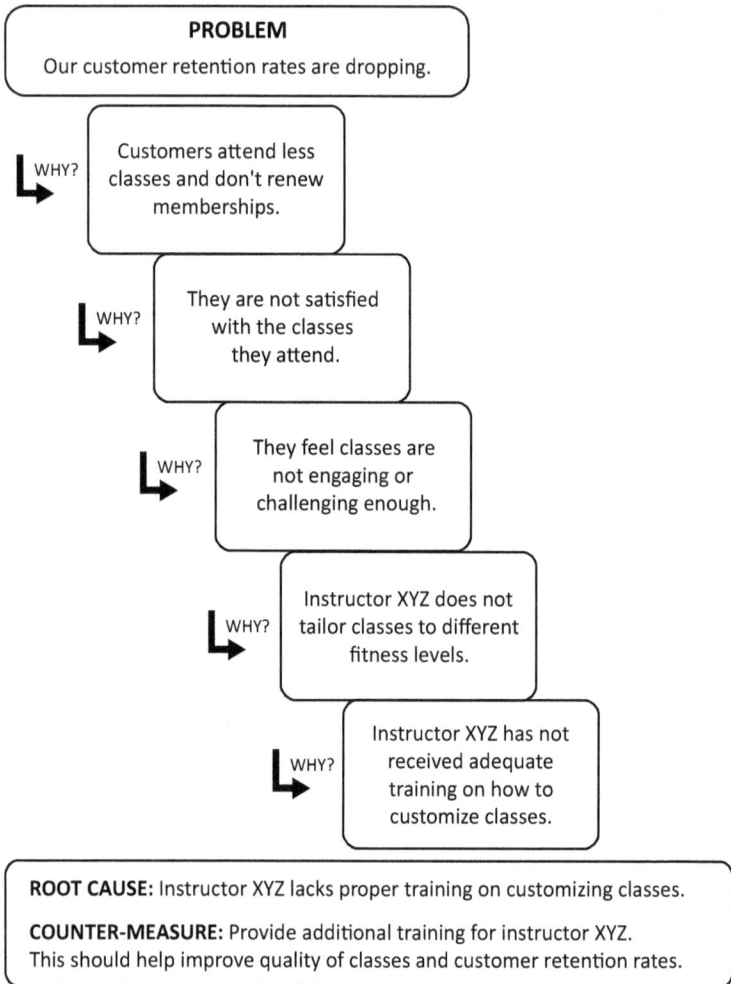

PROBLEM

Our customer retention rates are dropping.

WHY? Customers attend less classes and don't renew memberships.

WHY? They are not satisfied with the classes they attend.

WHY? They feel classes are not engaging or challenging enough.

WHY? Instructor XYZ does not tailor classes to different fitness levels.

WHY? Instructor XYZ has not received adequate training on how to customize classes.

ROOT CAUSE: Instructor XYZ lacks proper training on customizing classes.

COUNTER-MEASURE: Provide additional training for instructor XYZ.
This should help improve quality of classes and customer retention rates.

---

3. **Correlation**

This technique is used to identify relationships between two or more variables. It identifies how changes in one variable are associated with changes in another.

Continuing with our example, perhaps the instructor has noticed that attendance drops significantly on sunnier days. This would constitute a negative correlation between weather and class attendance.

Technically, a correlation analysis would consist of three pretty self-explanatory steps:

1. Data collection
2. Correlation coefficient calculation
3. Results analysis

Therefore, our instructor here would start by collecting data from the class attendance trackers and daily temperatures. They could then leverage statistical BI tools or software (i.e., Microsoft Excel, Tableau, R, etc) to calculate the correlation coefficient. This number would range from -1 to 1; suggesting the following:

- **Close to 1:** Strong positive correlation, both variables move in the same direction. For example: If the temperature increases, attendance also increases.

- **Close to -1:** Strong negative correlation, both variables moving in opposite directions. For example: If the temperature increases, attendance decreases.

- **Around 0:** No correlation. For example: The changes in temperature do not significantly affect attendance in any particular way.

Causation vs. Correlation

As we covered both causation (refer to explanation of root cause analysis, point 2) and correlation above, I believe it is important to clarify here that correlation does not imply causation, in the way that just because two things move together, it does not mean that one causes the other.

4. **Diagnostic Regression Analysis**

   Another powerful statistical technique in BI is to understand the relationship(s) between a dependent variable (y) and one or more independent variables (x). The idea is that it enables us to predict the value of "y" based on the values of "x," giving us a better idea of how different variables interact with each other, and how they influence the outcome.

In simple terms, if we were looking to identify the relationship between two variables, we would perform a "single linear regression" analysis, while it would be called "multiple regression" analysis if we were exploring three or more variables.

Without going too deep into this topic, I am adding Figure 4.5 below; a visual outline of the steps usually followed to perform this analysis. If you are curious to explore this further, I would suggest researching available resources online, like the "nature methods" journal.[10]

Figure 4.5   **An illustration of the diagnostic regression analysis steps**

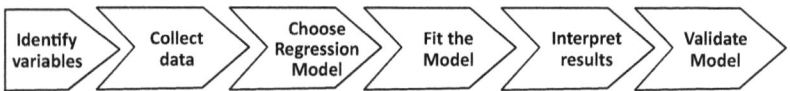

5. **Drill-down analysis**

The last technique we are going to cover here is frequently used to explore our data by breaking down the big-picture information into smaller, more specific parts. In terms of business intelligence, this method helps us understand the underlying details that make up trends and patterns.

Back to the pilates studio example, perhaps we have noticed that overall class attendance has been dropping recently. In this case, we could decide to perform a drill-down analysis to pinpoint specific issues behind this trend that we could

---

10. Nature Methods, "The coefficient of determination R² and intra-class correlation coefficient ICC," *Nature Methods 13* (2016): 419, https://www.nature.com

address accordingly. Figure 4.6 below offers an illustration of the steps we would need to follow and the data we could leverage for our example.

| Figure 4.6 | **An illustration of the drill-down analysis** |

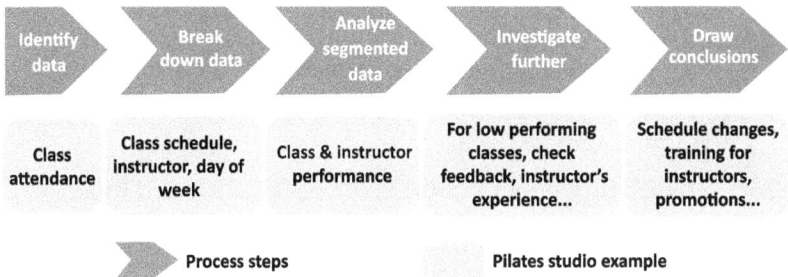

Identify data	Break down data	Analyze segmented data	Investigate further	Draw conclusions
Class attendance	Class schedule, instructor, day of week	Class & instructor performance	For low performing classes, check feedback, instructor's experience...	Schedule changes, training for instructors, promotions...

Process steps   Pilates studio example

4.2.2 Benefits of diagnostic analytics

When we learn about the "why" behind our data, we also unlock the following benefits:

- **Root cause identification:** We identify the underlying reasons behind specific outcomes and are better prepared to stop them from recurring.

- **Better problem-solving:** This process provides us with tools/techniques that we can incorporate into our usual practices, to implement more effective problem resolutions.

- **Predictive preparation:** By understanding "why" things happened, our business can transition to a more proactive mindset, anticipating similar issues that may occur in the future. We will dive deeper into this in Chapter Five.

- **Improved strategic planning:** With the help of insights and learnings we extract from implementing these techniques, we can refine our business strategies and decision-making processes.

4.2.3 Disadvantages of diagnostic analytics

The implementation of diagnostic analytics in BI can also have some disadvantages, such as:

- **Complexity:** It often requires more sophisticated tools and techniques. Therefore, less technical/experienced users could struggle initially.

- **Time-consuming:** Requires more time as the exercise of diving deeper into data relies on detailed data collection and thorough analysis.

- **Data quality dependency:** You might have heard this before but the concept of "Garbage In, Garbage Out" (GIGO) really rings true here; poor quality data will lead to inaccurate conclusions.

- **Potential for overfitting:** This refers to the risk of over-refining data and finding patterns that are too tailored for a specific dataset, and do not become applicable beyond that data.

In summary, through diagnostic analytics we delve deeper into our data to uncover root causes and understand why specific events are happening. While it increases the complexity of our BI process, it provides valuable insights that we would not be able to achieve by sticking to descriptive analytics.

4.3 Creating and Interpreting BI Reports

Now that you are familiar with both descriptive and diagnostic analytics, we can move on to a more exciting and practical topic: how to create and interpret BI reports. A lot has happened already in our BI journey to get to this stage, and now it is time to bring it all together so that others in the company can also benefit from all this work. The BI report will enable us to summarize and communicate insights and recommendations in a very digestible format.

Before we move forward with the practical steps of developing BI reports, I believe it will be beneficial to pause for a moment and address a subject that frequently causes confusion.

4.3.1 Report vs. dashboard in BI reporting

First, let's understand individual definitions of these concepts:

- **Report:** A detailed presentation that can include various charts and visualizations. It may cover a wide range of related information, or focus specifically on a single purpose or event. A report's main goal is to provide detailed intelligence on an organization's operations, often presenting data as a snapshot in time.[11]

- **Dashboard:** A tool for displaying key metrics and indicators in a way that can easily be digested at a glance. It aggregates important data and uses visual elements like scales, gauges, and traffic light-style indicators, to represent progress toward specific goals. Dashboards are designed to provide contextual insights and to support decision-making processes by presenting key metrics and performance in an intuitive format.[12]

With this in mind, we can explore the actual differences between them in detail. Find a summarized view in Table 4.1.

Table 4.1	Overview of differences between reports and dashboards

	Reports	Dashboards
Purpose	Very detailed analysis and information	Real-time performance monitoring and trend identification
Audience	Analysts and auditors	Executives and operational staff

---

11. Chartio, "Dashboards vs. Reports: How They're the Same, How They're Different," retrieved from https://chartio.com
12. Gartner, "Dashboard," retrieved from https://www.gartner.com

	Reports	Dashboards
Data Refresh	Periodic updates	Real-time data updates
Interactivity	Static and non-interactive	Highly interactive and dynamic
Usual Format	Long tables and charts, with written explanations	Single screen/page display, very limited narrative

By grasping these important differences between reports and dashboards, you will be more prepared to choose the most suitable tool for your requirements, depending on the specific objectives and needs of your BI strategy. Aligning the appropriate tool with the desired outcome is essential for making effective decisions, whether you are concentrating on detailed historical analysis or monitoring key metrics in real time.

Next, let's dive right into BI reporting and explore how to approach this practically.

4.3.2 Creating BI reports

Initially, you may struggle with reporting in BI as you may not be familiar with the reporting software, but I assure you it will be one of the most rewarding stages of this journey. Let's understand it by breaking it down into small milestones.

Before we dive in, I have prepared below an illustration of the steps we are about to cover in this section, so that you can get an initial helicopter view of the end-to-end process (see Figure. 4.7):

Figure 4.7 **Steps to create a BI report**

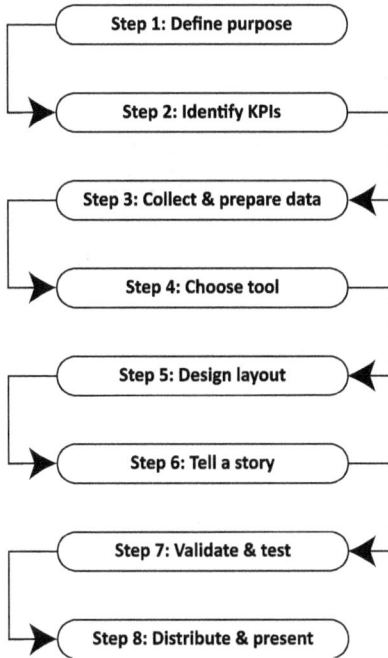

1. **Define the purpose of the report**

   The high-level purpose of a BI report is to summarize and provide actionable insights. However, for our report to truly be effective, we will need to dig one level deeper and understand what the report will be utilized for.

   To succeed with this task, we should always start by asking our stakeholders the right questions. Who are going to be the key users? What do they want to learn by using this report? What business problem/area are they trying to monitor?

2. **Identify key metrics**

   Next, we would begin the analytical process, and therefore proceed with the application of the initial stages we introduced when discussing descriptive analytics. If you need a refresher on KPIs, I would recommend revisiting the first step of section 4.1.1.

Quick Tips

A good practice when defining metrics is to apply the 'SMART' framework[13]; meaning that your metrics should be: Specific (clear and precise), Measurable (quantifiable), Attainable (realistic and achievable), Relevant (aligned with goals), and Time-bound (with a defined timeline). This will help ensure the KPIs you select are truly relevant and impactful.

---

3. **Collect and prepare data**

Now that we have identified our KPIs, the next step will be gathering data from relevant sources, as we saw in the second and third stages of section 4.1.1.

Here is where the GIGO concept, which we introduced earlier, comes into play. It is crucial not to rush this step and to prioritize achieving high-quality data. With this in mind, we will invest time in cleaning and transforming our data; which may involve items like correcting errors, dealing with blank cells, and removing duplicates.

4. **Choose the reporting tool**

Based on the guidance provided in Chapter Three, we will then move towards evaluating different reporting tools and choosing the one that best fulfills our requirements and/or unique circumstances surrounding our budget, ease of use, etc.

---

13. George T. Doran, "There's a S.M.A.R.T. Way to Write Management's Goals and Objectives," *Management Review* 70, no. 11 (1981): 35-36.

5. Design the report layout

With all the progress achieved through the previous steps, we can now roll up our sleeves and get hands-on with our report. Get those creative, visual-oriented parts of your brain ready, as they will come in handy for this task.

The first couple of times you develop a dashboard/report from scratch, you may experience the "Blank Page/Canvas Syndrome," a condition usually associated with writing, that one may suffer when starting a new project. This may result in you staring hopelessly at a blank screen.

We will cover the topic of designing report layouts in detail in Chapter Seven, but some high-level best practices we can already introduce here are:

- Follow a clean and uncluttered layout
- Use consistent color schemes and self-explanatory naming conventions
- Do not overdo it - include only what is important
- Choose the right visualization for your data

Additionally, if you would like to learn more about effective reporting design, I would highly recommend two resources: *"The Big Book of Dashboards: Visualizing Your Data Using Real-World Business Scenarios,"*[14] written collaboratively by authors Steve Wexler, Jeffrey Shaffer, and Andy Cotgreave; and the whitepaper *"Visual Analysis Best Practices: Simple Techniques for Making Every Data Visualization Useful and Beautiful,"*[15] created by the Tableau Software team and free to download.

---

14. Steve Wexler, Jeffrey Shaffer and Andy Cotgreave, The Big Book of Dashboards: Visualizing Your Data Using Real-World Business Scenarios. Hoboken, NJ: Wiley, 2017.

15. Jonathan Schwabish, Visual Analysis Best Practices, Simple Techniques for Making Every Data Visualization Useful and Beautiful, Washington, DC: Urban Institute Press, 2020.

6. Tell a story

Our BI report is taking shape, and now we want to make sure it follows a clear and logical structure; as well as a correct flow to guide stakeholders through our findings. For dashboards, a good practice to achieve this is placing key information from the top left corner to the right. For reports, it is recommended to start the document with an executive summary that highlights the key findings. A more detailed analysis can be provided for the reader later in the document, finishing with actionable recommendations, as shown in Figure 4.8.

Figure 4.8 **Representation of recommended dashboard/report layout**

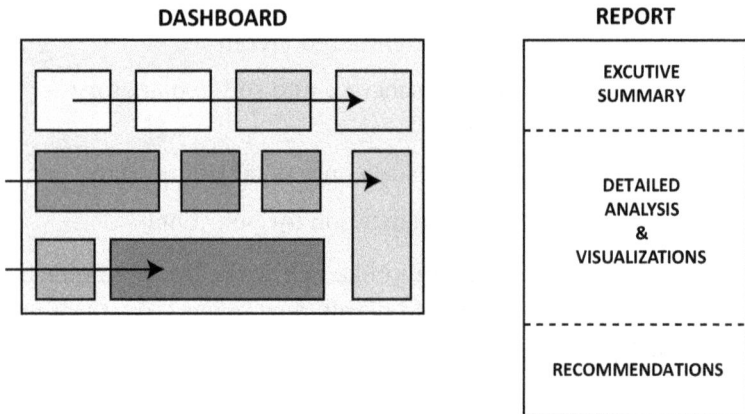

If you are interested in the power and impact of data storytelling, I would highly recommend the book *"Storytelling with Data: A Data Visualization Guide for Business Professionals,"*[16] by Cole Nussbaumer Knaflic. Even after all these years, I still find myself sometimes returning to this book when working on dashboards.

---

16. Cole Nussbaumer Knaflic, Storytelling with Data: A Data Visualization Guide for Business Professionals, Hoboken, NJ: Wiley, 2015.

7. Validate and test the report

Great, we have our BI reporting ready. However, before sharing it with our audience, we must take the time to review the data and visualizations, ensuring they work as expected and are accurate.

The last thing we want is to share the dashboard with our colleagues only to receive comments about the data inaccuracy, unclear/missing chart titles, or the visualizations not responding properly when interacted with. We only get one chance to launch this thing, and we want to ensure it is done right by double-checking that everything is polished and meets expectations.

8. Distribute and present

Next, you can share the report with the stakeholders identified in the first step. Here I recommend scheduling a walk-through session where you can personally show users how to access, interact with, and interpret the dashboard, especially if it is the first time you are developing one. During this session, you could also mention to stakeholders that they can come back to you with questions and feedback after the workshop, as they get more familiar with the report/dashboard.

Considering the time and hard work you have put into this BI solution, you want to make sure stakeholders feel comfortable using it, and more importantly, adopting it for their decision-making processes.

4.3.3 Interpreting BI Reports

While it is important that our solutions are being actively used, it is also crucial that stakeholders can digest and extract meaningful insights from them. Therefore, I suggest approaching this section of the Chapter with the same level of focus as the previous one.

Think about it. There would be very little value in allocating all that time to develop reports/dashboards if they were not helping us and our teams make better-informed decisions and operate more efficiently overall.

Find below guidance on how to interpret BI reports:

1. **Understanding the context of the metrics**

   To ensure we are interpreting our BI reports correctly, we must revisit the previous step of "identifying key metrics". Here, we would corroborate with our stakeholders that the metrics shown in the report are well understood, and how they are associated with business goals. The aim is to ensure that users comprehend correctly what each metric represents, and its relevance to the business.

2. **Start with a high-level overview**

   We then move on to looking at the big picture. What insights do we get when glancing at the BI report for the first time? Do not underestimate this initial check, as more often than not, it will give you ideas and valuable judgments about the current status of the business and guide you toward specific areas that might require further exploration.

3. **Identifying trends and patterns**

   Next, let's get a closer look at specific charts and data. Are they showing an upward or downward trend? Are there any outliers that deviate from the standard patterns? We could also explore performance across different timeframes, products, and geographies, and proceed to investigate discrepancies, if any.

   Depending on how the dashboard has been designed, users may have the functionality to drill down and explore underlying data. By leveraging this feature, they can gain a more granular understanding of any anomalies or significant changes.

4. Comparing against benchmarks

As we begin to understand the details behind specific trends and patterns, we can now examine this data from multiple angles. For instance, we could compare it against historical data, pre-established goals, performance in other business areas, and/or industry standards. This popular practice, known as benchmarking, allows us to identify areas for further improvement. For effective outcomes, it is key to first establish as a business/team what are relevant and realistic benchmarks for comparison.

5. Asking critical questions

Throughout the process of interpreting business intelligence reports, we should encourage stakeholders to actively ask themselves questions about the report and data while interacting with it. Additionally, we must foster close collaboration to gain diverse perspectives and to ensure the analysis and extracted insights are objective. This cross-functional engagement will likely lead to uncovering additional insights that may not have been obvious at first.

6. Taking action based on insights

Although this is quite an obvious step, it is still forgotten sometimes. The ultimate goal of all these efforts and hard work is to drive meaningful action. We want our users to walk away from the dashboards and reports with a clear understanding of how to proceed next and which areas to prioritize.

In fact, if we have developed the BI report from scratch, it is highly possible that after all the time spent iterating the dashboard/report and making sense of the data, we will be able to directly identify some actionable recommendations. If this is the case, it can be a good practice to directly present those recommendations to our shareholders when sharing the BI report.

Once the course of action is agreed upon and teams start its implementation, we should monitor the impact of these actions on the observed trends and patterns. By continuously evaluating this, we will better understand how specific actions affect the performance of our KPIs and ensure the team is moving in the right direction.

4.3.4 Practical example

I would like to bring it all together for you with a practical example. I am giving our Pilates instructor a break and switching to a business that might not traditionally come from a very data-driven industry. However, I believe showcasing this type of business will demonstrate more clearly how every organization, regardless of their size or industry, can benefit from the power of data and reporting.

With this in mind, let me introduce our Pet Daycare Center.

You are now part of the management team of a pet daycare center and you are leading a project to improve the center's operations by leveraging BI reports. Before starting development, you meet with the rest of the management team and align on the KPIs that will help you to understand what is currently impacting your operational performance and revenue. Some of the metrics you define are: occupancy rates, customer retention rates, revenue per service for daycare, training, grooming services, and booking cancellation rates.

Once this is clear, you explore the available data sources and pinpoint those that will provide the required data to track the agreed KPIs. Some of these are: booking systems, customer databases, financial records, and social media.

With all the data ready, sorted, and prepared for analysis, you realize you need to choose the reporting tool, as this is the first time the team is going to be implementing this type of reporting. Knowing the available budget and number of users, you first consider Tableau or Power BI but decide to move forward with the latter one to guarantee an easier integration with the rest of the applications used at the center.

It is now time to get creative. Remembering the good practices you have learned, you focus on creating a clean, uncluttered dashboard that highlights the most critical KPIs at the top. You also know that for this solution to be truly impactful, the data needs to tell a story. Therefore, you also build a report with an executive summary that features key findings such as: a 10% increase in weekly occupancy rates, and a 15% increase in booking cancellations.

After that, you outline the individual findings on other KPIs to provide more detailed context. In the dashboard, you prepare some interactive visualizations to show occupancy trends and cancellation patterns with line charts, and revenue changes with a bar chart per service; now you include some key insights from this analysis into the report. At the end of the report, you also suggest some recommendations you have identified while working with the data. For example, you recommend adjusting staffing during peak times and offering promotions to increase customer retention.

After cross-checking the data and testing that the dashboard works as expected, you arrange a session with the management team where you not only share access to the tool, but also walk them through the report and the interactive functionalities of the dashboard. While reviewing the report together, you all start identifying some areas for improvement. You realize that pet occupancy rates are higher on Wednesdays and Thursdays, that grooming has become the least profitable branch of the business, and that customer retention rates are higher for training services but lower for daycare.

Based on these insights, you then spend some time developing an action plan for the next three months before closing the session. You will jointly review this action plan every two weeks and assess how it impacts the trends observed in the dashboard.

4.4 Case Studies

I am optimistic that you enjoyed the pets daycare center example and that it helped to synthesize all the new concepts we have introduced in the Chapter. Now, I would like to present some real-world case studies showcasing successful implementations of descriptive and diagnostic analytics:

Table 4.2	Overview of descriptive and diagnostic analytics case studies
Descriptive Analytics	
Netflix has admitted employing descriptive analytics to analyze data from their customers, in order to pinpoint which TV shows and movies are trending at any given time. By reviewing its users' consumption habits, the company can identify popular content and feature it prominently on its platform.	Walmart is another known user of descriptive analytics, which they leverage to analyze sales data, buyers' preferences, and consumption patterns. This helps the company streamline inventory management, optimize its supply chain organization, and tailor marketing strategies to customer needs.
Diagnostic Analytics	
General Electric (GE) leverages this branch of BI analytics to identify the root causes of machinery failures and production inefficiencies. This approach helps them improve their maintenance schedules, reduce downtime, and enhance the reliability of their equipment.	JPMorgan Chase also employs diagnostic analytics to investigate the reasons behind financial anomalies and fraud incidents. This way, they are empowered to enhance their fraud detection systems while mitigating financial risks, and improving their regulatory compliance.

Chapter Summary

◆ Descriptive analytics helps us understand what has happened in the past, using data to identify trends and patterns and is essential for effective decision-making and reporting.

◆ Diagnostic analytics enables us to delve deeper and understand why certain trends or patterns occur, using techniques such as hypothesis testing, root cause analysis, and correlation.

◆ Creating effective BI reports involves defining the report's purpose, identifying key metrics, and collecting and preparing data. This is followed by choosing the right reporting tool, designing the report layout, telling a story with the data, and validating and presenting the report.

◆ Interpreting BI reports requires understanding the context of the metrics, starting with a high-level overview, identifying trends and patterns, comparing against benchmarks, asking critical questions, and taking action based on insights.

Quiz

1. **What is the primary goal of descriptive analytics?**
   a. Predicting future outcomes
   b. Understanding past and present data
   c. Prescribing actions to achieve desired results
   d. Automating decision-making processes

2. **Which of the following is a key component of a BI report?**
   a. Data mining algorithms
   b. High-level overview
   c. Predictive modeling
   d. Machine learning

3. **What technique is used to identify the root cause of a problem by repeatedly asking "why"?**
   a. Correlation analysis
   b. Regression analysis
   c. 5 Whys
   d. Hypothesis testing

4. **Which metric is an example of a KPI for a retail store?**
   a. Number of sunny days
   b. Monthly sales revenue
   c. Global stock prices
   d. Email open rates

5. **What is the difference between correlation and causation?**

   a. Correlation implies causation

   b. Correlation shows a relationship, and causation shows a direct effect

   c. Causation implies correlation

   d. Correlation and causation are the same

6. **Which type of analysis involves comparing current data against historical data?**

   a. Predictive analysis

   b. Diagnostic analysis

   c. Descriptive analysis

   d. Prescriptive analysis

7. **What is the purpose of hypothesis testing in diagnostic analytics?**

   a. To predict future trends

   b. To determine the validity of a hypothesis

   c. To automate data collection

   d. To visualize data patterns

8. **Which of the following is an example of using descriptive analytics in a retail store?**

   a. Forecasting future sales based on past trends

   b. Analyzing monthly sales data to identify best-selling products

   c. Recommending products to customers based on their preferences

   d. Automating inventory restocking processes

9. **What does SMART stand for in defining KPIs?**

   a. Simple, Measurable, Achievable, Realistic, Timely

   b. Specific, Measurable, Attainable, Relevant, Time-bound

   c. Strategic, Measurable, Attainable, Relevant, Testable

   d. Specific, Manageable, Achievable, Realistic, Timely

10. **What is the first step in creating a BI report?**

   a. Designing the report layout

   b. Defining the purpose of the report

   c. Collecting and preparing data

   d. Choosing the reporting tool

Answers	1 – b	2 – b	3 – c	4 – b	5 – b
	6 – c	7 – b	8 – b	9 – b	10 – b

Chapter 5

Predictive Analytics and Forecasting

KEY LEARNING OBJECTIVES

- Understand the concept and power of predictive analytics.
- Get familiar with the key components involved.
- Explore the most common techniques for predictive analytics.
- Learn the steps required for its implementation.
- Review real-world applications.

Next stop, Predictive Analytics. Now that we know what happened and why, in this chapter, we will explore how to leverage business intelligence to look forward and use data to anticipate what might happen next. We will follow a very similar structure to the previous chapter. First, we shall get familiar with this branch of analytics, to then explore common techniques and methods for implementation, and finish with some real-life examples.

5.1 Introduction to Predictive Analytics

As described by Harvard Business School,[17] "Predictive analytics is the use of data to predict future trends and events. It uses historical data to forecast potential scenarios that can help drive strategic decisions." You may think this sounds a bit too magical, almost like having a crystal ball for your business. However, the reality is there are a lot of statistics and advanced analytics techniques involved to arrive at this point.

The process of implementing predictive analytics in business intelligence is usually broken down into five key steps, which may look familiar to you as the high-level overview is very similar to what we saw in the previous chapter for some of the diagnostic analytics techniques (see Fig 5.1).

Figure 5.1   **An illustration of the steps for predictive analytics in BI**

| Problem definition | Data gathering & preparation | Data pre-processing | Predictive model development | Results validation & deployment |

1. **Problem definition**

   Similar to the diagnostic analytics technique, our very first step here will be to identify the problem we are aiming to solve through this process. We need to be very clear about the business objective/goal this will relate to, and the specific questions we are trying to answer through our BI project.

   Since we have already explored examples related to a Pilates studio and a pet daycare center, I will move into one of my other big passions to illustrate these five steps: traveling.

---

17. Harvard Business School Online, "Predictive Analytics: What It Is & Why It Matters," retrieved from https://online.hbs.edu

We are now a smart travel agent and we have decided to leverage the power of predictive analytics in BI to dive deep into the following matter: "How can we predict the most popular travel destinations for the next holiday season?" In other words, our objective is to forecast travel trends so we can then optimize marketing strategies and available offers.

2. Data gathering and preparation

With our business objective clearly defined, we can now start gathering all the relevant historical data that will provide context to the problem at hand. Exactly as we saw in Chapter Four, we will explore all the different data sources available and leverage those that help us get a complete view of this particular matter. And remembering the "Garbage In, Garbage Out (GIGO)" framework also introduced earlier in the book, we would want to spend some time here to ensure that the data is accurate, relevant, and comprehensive.

For our travel agency, this data might be found in booking records, previous seasonal trends, customer demographics, social media metrics, and even external sources like weather tracking and economic indices.

3. Data pre-processing

The raw data collected in the previous step will now require some work before it can be correctly leveraged for our predictive BI use case. Depending on the state of this data, some of the necessary steps may include: removing anomalies, addressing extreme outliers, and completing or removing any missing data points. In essence, we are getting our data into a suitable format before proceeding with the analysis.

As travel agents, this part of the process could consist of eliminating duplicate entries in our booking records, standardizing date and customer ID formats to achieve consistency, and taking care of missing data in our customers' profiles.

4. Predictive model development

We are now getting into the core of predictive analytics within the BI framework, and thus moving into steps more specifically related to this type of analysis. Here is where the magic happens, or rather where the statistics and advanced analysis mentioned earlier would come into play. In real-world applications, data scientists often employ tools and techniques already available to implement this step; which we will cover in the next section of this chapter.

Without spoiling too much of what will come later, we could say that for our travel agency, we would use our historical booking data to build and train the model that will predict the number of bookings we are likely to receive in the upcoming months.

5. Results validation and deployment

At this stage, we would want to dedicate time to validate both the predictive model and its results, before sharing them with our stakeholders. It is key that we are confident in their accuracy, as these insights will drive real-world decisions and strategies.

This validation step ensures the model is fit to reliably forecast future performance. Multiple iterations may be required as part of the model training process, until the solution is ready for deployment in our BI system.

As travel agents, once we have completed the validation of the predictive model, we can use recent booking details to assess the accuracy of its output. By comparing the model's forecasts against actual booking trends observed over that same period, we can evaluate the model's reliability.

For example, if the model forecasts an increase in bookings during the upcoming holiday season, we can then cross-reference that against the actual booking data from the same period. If the model's predictions are indeed closely aligned with the observed trends, this would serve as a strong indication of the model's reliability.

Once we have reached the desired level of reliability, we would then proceed to the deployment phase, meaning that we would integrate it into our usual booking system to receive real-time forecasts. These predictions could then be used to optimize how we run our agency; i.e., adjust marketing campaigns, amend our staffing schedule, modify our destination offering, and so on. An interesting remark here is that we should continue feeding more and more data into our model, which will be used to continue validating its predictions and its training. As a result, its reliability and accuracy can progressively increase over time, simultaneously improving the overall effectiveness of our BI approach.

5.2 Common Techniques

Now that you know more about the models underpinning predictive analytics, I am quite confident I have piqued your curiosity about what these models actually look like and how they are built. If this is true, let's not lose the momentum and explore this in greater depth. Generally speaking, predictive analytics models are split into two categories: classification and regression.

5.2.1 Classification models

As the name suggests, classification models aim to categorize or group data into predefined buckets or classes. Some simple examples of their application include spam email detection, credit scoring, and medical diagnosis. The classification they perform can be either binary, where there are only two predefined buckets including spam/not spam, high risk/low risk; or they can be multi-class, where multiple categories exist such as movie genres, colors, customer segments, or product types.

The key differentiation between classification and regression models is that the former attempts to predict a specific category rather than a continuous numerical value. They digest all the historical data we provide and leverage it to make a decision about which predefined bucket the new data should be assigned to.

Returning to our travel agency example, we could use classification models to predict whether a customer will book another trip with us within the next quarter (i.e., return/no return). Following the steps outlined earlier in this chapter, we would first gather and prepare all relevant data such as customer bookings, their demographics, and previous interactions with us. We could then explore which specific statistical algorithm[18] would best suit our use case and split our dataset into training and testing sets; which we would use to train and validate our model. For example, Logistic Regression is an algorithm commonly used for classification tasks.

Finally, once we have confirmed the model's reliability, we could integrate it with live data from our booking system, and use it to predict whether specific customers will return to us or not, in the short term. We could then utilize these insights about our customers to implement targeted retention strategies for those customers who are not likely to hire our services again.

---

18. In this book, we will not delve into specific statistical algorithms for predictive/preventive modeling. However, if you are eager to explore this topic further, you could read books like *"Introduction to Statistical Learning"* by Gareth James, Daniela Witten, Trevor Hastie, and Robert Tibshirani. If you prefer online learning, platforms like Coursera and DataCamp offer a vast variety of courses with comprehensive guides and hands-on exercises.

5.2.2 Regression models

In Chapter Four, we introduced basic regression concepts when exploring diagnostic analytics. Now, we will apply a different lens and learn how this powerful tool can also be utilized for predictive purposes.

Without going too deep into the underlying statistics, I will share an overview here of some of the most common regression modeling techniques. Since some of these new concepts might be tricky to comprehend at first, I will also include a visual representation for each of them at the end of this section.

Let's begin:

1. **Regression analysis**

   As discussed earlier, regression analysis is a statistical technique that estimates the direction and strength of relationships between variables. This way, we are able to understand how one variable changes when the other related variable also changes. For diagnostic analytics, the primary aim would be to identify the relationships between variables and the root causes influencing them *(explain "what" happened and "why")*. However, when used for predictive purposes, the technique applied varies slightly. Predictive models can forecast future outcomes by using those identified relationships *("what could" happen)*.

   Back to our role as travel agents, this technique would allow us to estimate the amount of bookings we may receive next month, based on factors such as social media advertising and seasonal trends. With the help of a relevant statistical model such as linear regression, we would be able to measure how these specific factors influence our customer demand. With that, we could then use our current advertising spend and seasonal information to generate forecasts of expected future bookings.

2. Decision trees

This particular technique can be applied both for classification and regression modeling. The process involves splitting the data into branches to illustrate the possible outcomes of specific decisions. This technique is very popular due to its simplicity and interpretability; decision trees are very easy to represent graphically, allowing less technical users to also digest their insights.

As travel agents, we could use decision trees to predict the revenue we will earn from each customer, based on their demographic characteristics and the trips they tend to book with us. The tree would examine all the different factors available such as customer age, preferred destination, etc. It would then identify those that are more relevant for predicting revenue; which are often referred to as the "root" of the tree.

The process would then start splitting the data multiple times into various categorizations or "branches," eventually reaching the end of each branch, which is the "leaf," where data cannot be divided any further. These leaf nodes would represent the final predicted revenue values. Once the tree is ready, we could start applying it right away. Let's say we get a new customer later that day with a specific destination in mind. Knowing their demographic details and the desired trip, we could look at our tree, follow the branches, and quickly check the forecasted revenue for that booking.

3. Neural networks

As the name suggests, this is an advanced technique that emulates how our brain functions and allows the identification of non-linear, complex relationships between variables. Essentially, this model creates multiple layers of interconnected nodes, where each of these nodes represents a junction of multiple inputs, and returns an individual numerical value.

For example, in the case of our travel agency, this model could be implemented to provide personalized experiences to our customers. We could feed historical data about our trip offerings, customers' past bookings, and social media engagement into the neural network and use it to identify patterns and preferences unique to each customer. This would empower us to offer them customized trips, experiences, and packages that they are likely to enjoy. Simultaneously, this enhanced customer service could also help us improve satisfaction scores and customer return rates, as they would feel more valued and attached to our agency.

4. **Time series analysis**

This last technique is significantly different from the ones we have covered previously. Time series analysis is very frequently used in businesses like travel agencies, as it is able to identify and predict time-related patterns. In other words, this technique enables us to forecast specific seasonalities for our business and their impact on metrics like revenue and number of bookings.

Thus, by implementing this analytical method, we would know in advance when we will have a busy period for bookings and adjust our trip offerings and staffing accordingly. This will ensure we are better prepared and can respond to the busy periods efficiently.

For an illustration of these four regression models, see below Figure 5.2:

Figure 5.2 **A visual representation of regression models**

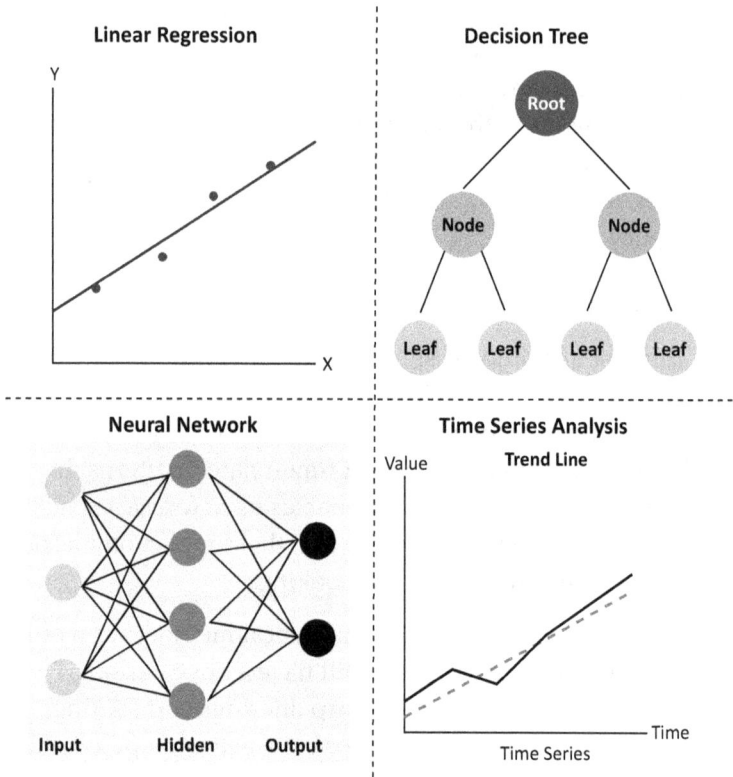

5.3 Implementing Predictive Models in BI Tools

Now that you are more familiar with the concept of predictive analytics, key techniques within this field, and the level of detail and insight you can gather through them, you have probably realized how powerful these models can be. They ensure you bring proactivity into your business and stay ahead of the curve.

Leveraging the BI report we built in Chapter Four, we can now enhance our solution by integrating predictive analytics and allowing our users to get more advanced and actionable insights. Even if this does not sound like much, by doing this, we will be changing how our teams operate; allowing them to adopt a more proactive approach, rather than just reacting to past events.

Considering we have already chosen the BI tool to use and connected it to the relevant data sources for our business goals, as covered in Chapters Three, Four, and Five, we would only need to follow four more steps to implement predictive analytics:

1. Developing the predictive model

This step requires some statistical knowledge to ensure we select the right model for our particular use case. Through this step, we would apply the required algorithms and train our model with historical data. Some popular tools used for this step are Azure Machine Learning and IBM Watson.

2. Deploying the model

Once the model is ready and trained, we would need to connect it with our existing BI tool so that it has access to real-time data and starts providing predictions.

3. Enhancing the interactive dashboard

With the model already able to generate predictions, we would definitely want to ensure we are allowing our users to access them, so that they can be used to inform our decisions and priorities moving forward. Thus, we would create some new visualizations that our colleagues can access and that display the predicted outcomes and their impact on business goals.

4. Validating and iterating

Lastly, it is crucial that we spend some time validating how the model performs with new data, and the accuracy of its predictions. Adjustments and iterations to the model might be required, to ensure that the model remains reliable and actionable over time.

Figure 5.3   **An overview of the practical implementation of predictive analytics**

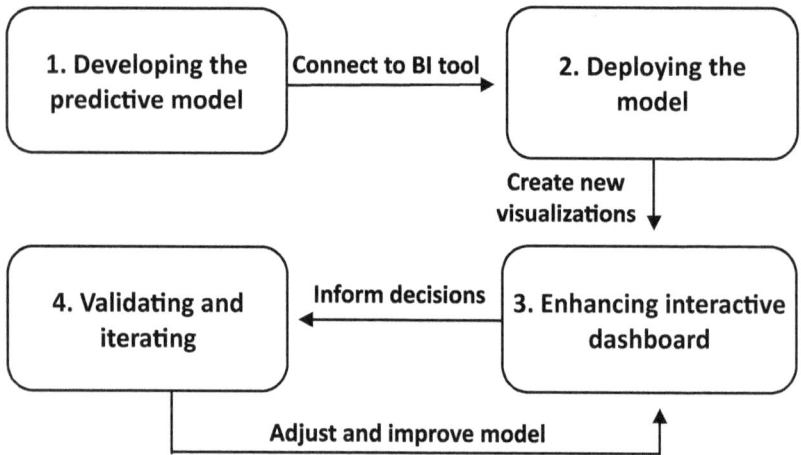

5.4 Case Studies

Let's review some successful real-world implementations of predictive analytics:

Table 5.1	Overview of predictive analytics case studies

Retail Industry	Manufacturing Industry
Amazon is known for analyzing their customers' purchase history and their item ratings to identify specific patterns and predict what products they could be interested in buying next.	Rolls-Royce collects real-time data from sensors on their infrastructure and connects it to machine learning models and algorithms. This allows them to identify anomalies and predict when components are likely to fail. This practice is usually known as preventive maintenance.
Weather Forecasting	**Formula 1**
Organizations like the UK Met Office are able to predict weather conditions by applying predictive analytics techniques that analyze patterns in historical weather. They also leverage this historical data to run simulations by validating and iterating data, and improving the accuracy of their predictions.	The Mercedes-AMG Petronas F1 Teams are also regular adopters of predictive analytics models, which they use to optimize their race strategy. Gathering real-time data from multiple sources such as car sensors, weather conditions, and driver performance, to predict the optimal times for pit stops.

Chapter Summary

◆ Predictive analytics is crucial for forecasting future trends and events, enabling businesses to anticipate changes and make informed decisions.

◆ Implementing predictive analytics involves five key steps: defining the problem, gathering and preparing data, pre-processing data, developing the predictive model, and validating and deploying the results.

◆ Common techniques in predictive analytics include classification models, regression models, decision trees, neural networks, and time series analysis.

◆ Integrating predictive models into BI tools enhances our interactive dashboards with actionable insights, allowing for real-time decision-making and strategy optimization.

Quiz

1. **What is the primary purpose of predictive analytics?**
   a. To describe past data
   b. To predict future trends and events
   c. To collect data
   d. To clean data

2. **Which of the following is the first step in implementing predictive analytics?**
   a. Data gathering
   b. Data pre-processing
   c. Problem definition
   d. Results validation

3. **Why is data pre-processing important in predictive analytics?**
   a. To collect data
   b. To clean and prepare data for analysis
   c. To predict future trends
   d. To validate results

4. **In the context of predictive analytics, what is a classification model used for?**
   a. Predicting numerical values
   b. Categorizing data into predefined classes
   c. Cleaning data
   d. Gathering data

5. **Which technique is used to identify and predict time-related patterns?**

   a. Regression analysis

   b. Decision trees

   c. Neural networks

   d. Time series analysis

6. **What is the key difference between diagnostic and predictive regression analysis?**

   a. Diagnostic focuses on historical data, predictive forecasts future outcomes

   b. Predictive focuses on historical data, diagnostic forecasts future outcomes

   c. Both are the same

   d. None of the above

7. **How do decision trees function in predictive analytics?**

   a. By categorizing data into predefined classes

   b. By splitting data into branches to illustrate possible outcomes

   c. By predicting time-related patterns

   d. By creating layers of interconnected nodes

8. **What is the role of neural networks in predictive analytics?**

   a. To categorize data

   b. To predict numerical values

   c. To identify non-linear, complex relationships between variables

   d. To gather data

9. **Which predictive analytics technique is commonly used in businesses like travel agencies to forecast specific seasonalities?**

   a. Regression analysis

   b. Decision trees

   c. Neural networks

   d. Time series analysis

10. **What is a crucial step before deploying a predictive model in a BI tool?**

    a. Collecting data

    b. Validating the model and its results

    c. Cleaning data

    d. Gathering data

Answers	1 – b	2 – c	3 – b	4 – b	5 – d
	6 – a	7 – b	8 – c	9 – a	10 – b

This page is intentionally left blank

Chapter **6**

Prescriptive Analytics and Optimization

KEY LEARNING OBJECTIVES

- Understand the concept and power of prescriptive analytics.
- Get familiar with key components involved.
- Explore the most common techniques for optimization.
- Learn steps required for the implementation of prescriptive analytics.
- Review real-world examples.

Up to this point, we have learnt how to make use of our historical data to develop basic descriptive BI reporting, and how to then enhance it with more advanced analytics: diagnostic and predictive. The combination of these three layers of analytics allows us to explore what has happened in the past and to forecast what might happen next. However, we still have one more level of analytics left to examine; a very powerful one I would say. This fourth type of analysis will enable us to identify the best course of action and the best strategy to achieve our goals.

6.1 Introduction to Prescriptive Analytics

Leveraging Gartner Glossary[19] again, we can describe prescriptive analytics as "a form of advanced analytics which examines data or content to answer the question *'What should be done?'* or *'What can we do to make _____ happen?'* It is characterized by techniques such as graph analysis, simulation, complex event processing, neural networks, recommendation engines, heuristics, and machine learning."

Simply put, in the context of business intelligence, prescriptive analytics is like having a Global Positioning System (GPS) for your business; one that not only tells you where you are and where you are going, but also guides you on the best route to get there.

6.1.1 The prescriptive analytics process

There are multiple factors involved in determining the optimal route, and its implementation can vary depending on specific business objectives. To keep things simple, let's explore the end-to-end process, represented in Figure 6.1 below.

Figure 6.1   **An illustration of how prescriptive analytics work**

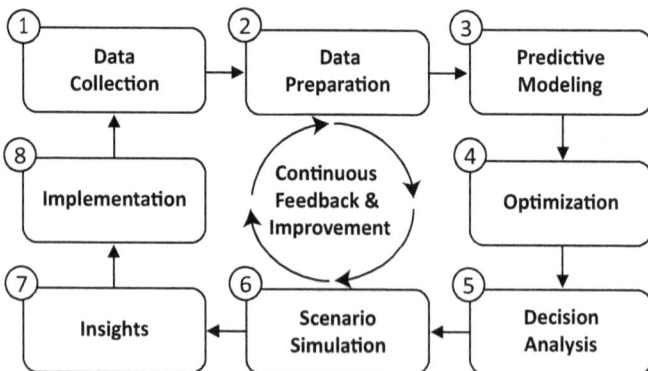

---

19. Gartner, "Prescriptive Analytics," retrieved from https://www.gartner.com

Note: Since you are already familiar with the first three steps (Data Collection and Data Preparation - Chapter Four, section 4.1; Predictive Modeling - Chapter Five, section 5.1), we will jump directly into step four.

1. Optimization

To ensure the best solution is selected for our BI system, the mere deployment of a predictive model (as discussed in Chapter Five, section 5.3) is not sufficient. This is where "Optimization," a branch of mathematics and computer science, typically comes into play. It consists of the application of techniques to identify the best possible solution from the set of predictions and proposed actions suggested by the predictive model. We will explore some of these optimization techniques in more detail later in this chapter.

2. Decision analysis

To assess as many potential decisions and scenarios as possible, decision analysis uses a systematic and quantitative approach. This tool integrates the results from the optimization step with business priorities and challenges. It combines probability theory, statistics and psychology to support decision-makers assess uncertainties. By comparing the forecasted results for each alternative, it pinpoints the one that yields the best outcome. Some of the most common methods used for decision analysis are: decision trees, cost-benefit analysis and multi-criteria decision analysis.

3. Scenario simulation

This step consists of creating and analyzing various possible scenarios to comprehend the potential consequences and outputs of each decision under multiple conditions. This approach is particularly impactful within the BI framework in areas characterized by high uncertainty, such as business strategy and climate science. We will revisit and examine this step in greater depth later in this chapter.

4. **Insights**

As mentioned throughout this book, the ultimate purpose of business intelligence is to generate meaningful and actionable insights from the available data. The execution of prescriptive analytics enables teams to accurately extract these insights and recommendations, which can then be effectively presented and shared with relevant stakeholders to highlight the best next steps forward.

5. **Implementation**

Now that we know how to proceed, there is only one thing left to do: execute. The implementation phase involves executing the plans, strategies, and/or recommendations generated by prescriptive analytics. Effective implementation and monitoring are crucial for the success of our BI initiatives; thus, I have included a dedicated section on this topic later in the chapter.

6.1.2 Benefits

The key advantage of prescriptive analytics within a business intelligence context is understanding the best future steps and their potential outcome for our business, but it is not the only benefit.

Some other benefits of its implementation are:

- **Resources optimization:** By following data-driven recommendations, prescriptive analytics enables us to improve resource allocation and operational efficiencies.

- **Competitive advantage:** While making better and faster decisions, we are also gaining a competitive edge.

- **Risk mitigation:** This approach allows teams to be proactive against potential risks, while also suggesting preventive measures for their mitigation.

6.1.3 Disadvantages

Prescriptive analytics can also come with some drawbacks such as:

- **Complexity:** The implementation of this branch of analytics requires knowledge of complex algorithms and models, as well as an understanding of optimization techniques. Thus, the business might need to either invest in specialized support or in upskilling their employees, before the implementation of prescriptive analytic methods.

- **High cost:** Due to the advanced techniques and methods integrated within prescriptive analytics, its implementation might require a higher investment in technology and infrastructure.

- **Data quality dependency:** Circling back to the GIGO concept mentioned in previous chapters, the quality of the insights and recommendations generated by this methodology will also depend on the quality of the input data.

In conclusion, prescriptive analytics undoubtedly brings significant advantages to our business and teams. However, it is important to remember that its implementation will also come with certain challenges. Therefore, it is key that before beginning its implementation, we carefully assess the purpose and expectations with our teams. This way, we can evaluate potential disadvantages, and work towards overcoming them. If we go through the process and effort of implementing prescriptive analytics as part of our BI initiative, we want to make sure we are ready to maximize the benefits it can provide.

6.2 Optimization and Simulation Techniques for BI

As discussed earlier, optimization and simulation are two key methodologies in BI when it comes to prescriptive analytics. Given their importance, it will be beneficial to cover them in more detail, providing you with a foundational understanding of some of the most frequent techniques used for their deployment.

6.2.1 Optimization techniques

If you remember from section 6.1.1, optimization allows us to find the best possible solution from a range of alternatives, by leveraging mathematical algorithms.

Let's look at the three most commonly used optimization techniques:

1. **Linear programming:** This approach consists of optimizing, by either minimizing or maximizing a linear objective function, based on our business goals. Now, in plain English, we could define it as the method to find the best outcome, where we can adjust some variables while respecting some fixed rules or constraints.

   For instance, we would use linear programming to identify the specific amount of products (variables) that would allow us to maximize profit (objective), without exceeding our storage capacity (fixed rule/constraint).

2. **Integer programming:** This is a very similar technique to the one covered above, but where the variables are always whole numbers, without decimals (integer values). For example, we could use integer programming to calculate the exact number of trucks to hire for our deliveries (variable), which would allow us to minimize freight costs (objective) while sticking to our budget (constraint).

3. **Nonlinear programming:** This technique is slightly more complex, as in this case, the variables do not share a linear

relationship. For example, a good application for this technique could be if we wanted to define the optimal amount of funds to invest in various assets (variables) to maximize our profits (objective), without surpassing our risk tolerance (constraint).

6.2.2 Simulation techniques

This approach would also allow us to find the best feasible alternative, but in this case by developing a model of real-world scenarios and experimenting with them to understand their potential consequences and results.

The three most popular simulation techniques are:

1. **Monte Carlo simulation:** This technique heavily relies on statistics to calculate the probability of each possible outcome. It enables us to see what could happen in the future, and it does so by running multiple simulations with different inputs.

   This technique is often used for financial modeling. For instance, it would allow us to estimate the future value of our investment portfolio, by simulating multiple scenarios with different interest rates.

2. **Discrete event simulation:** In this case, the simulations are run for a chain of events that happen at specific times; where events occur one after another and can individually impact the outcome. For example, this technique could be very useful to optimize the number and flow of patients in the emergency room of a hospital. It could model the arrival and treatment of these patients, and estimate the optimal number of doctors and nurses that should be on duty during each shift.

3. **Agent-based modeling:** In this case, the variables or agents are independent of one another, but they can all interact between them and impact the final outcome. A practical use

case for this technique could be the exploration of how new traffic policies could affect the traffic in our city. The model would simulate the new behavior and circulation dynamics of the individual drivers (agents), and calculate the impact on traffic based on existing factors like road capacity, speed limits, and amount of traffic lights.

Before moving on to the next section, there is something I would like to clarify. The techniques covered here both for Optimization and Simulation are very powerful but also quite advanced. Therefore, if you are feeling overwhelmed right now, that is perfectly normal. Undoubtedly, it takes time and effort to master these techniques, and it is not expected to reach that level immediately, or ever, depending on your needs. The key expected takeaway here is to have a foundational understanding of what these techniques are and what they can do.

Whenever you feel ready or curious enough to delve deeper into the world of analytics and some of the more advanced techniques, having this basic knowledge will be a valuable starting point. Thus, my main goal here is to provide you with a strong introduction, so that when the time comes to explore this further, you have a clearer sense of their potential applications and benefits.

6.3 Implementing Prescriptive Models in BI Tools

As is also the case for the wider BI framework, the predictive and prescriptive branches of data analytics will ultimately pursue the optimization of decision-making processes, while they continuously improve and learn from the outcomes of the actions they suggest.

However, there are also two fundamental differences between both approaches, that I believe are relevant to highlight here:

- Predictive analytics fundamentally concentrates on providing forecasted results, whereas Prescriptive analytics centers more heavily on recommending specific actions to take.

- Prescriptive analytics will leverage optimization techniques, which are not part of the framework for predictive analytics.

Having clarified these differences, let's review the practical implementation of prescriptive analytics through a simple made-up example of a theme park:

Figure 6.2   **An overview of the implementation of prescriptive analytics**

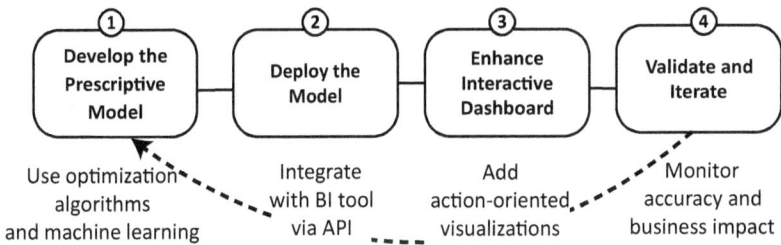

① Develop the Prescriptive Model	② Deploy the Model	③ Enhance Interactive Dashboard	④ Validate and Iterate
Use optimization algorithms and machine learning	Integrate with BI tool via API	Add action-oriented visualizations	Monitor accuracy and business impact

1. Developing the prescriptive model

Let's imagine we are part of the project team responsible for implementing a prescriptive analytics-powered BI system for a widely known theme park in our country. Here, the ultimate goal is to optimize the experience for park visitors.

We have indeed gotten this far in the book with our team, and let's assume, we have already implemented everything that has been covered in previous chapters. This means we have a functioning BI reporting tool so far, that allows users to check and understand previous performance and current trends. It also provides some predictions about the expected occupancy levels and ride popularity at the park for the upcoming months.

Thus, our next step will be to create a model that generates specific recommendations for the theme park coordinators, to adopt and optimize their operations. This way, they will be able to efficiently manage their available resources while maximizing their visitors' satisfaction. As seen earlier in this chapter, for this purpose we would leverage optimization algorithms to develop the required prescriptive model. This model would consider variables and inputs like: ride capacity, staff availability, and weather forecasts, along with historical, real-time, and predicted occupancy levels.

2. **Deploying the model**

   With our model now prepared, we integrate it directly with our BI tool of choice so that our tool and model remain seamlessly connected, continuously interchanging data. The BI system would feed the park's operational data into the model, which would then send back its recommended actions to be surfaced through our reporting.

3. **Enhancing our interactive dashboard**

   Once the model is deployed, we proceed to create new visualizations in our BI dashboard. These visualizations enable us to show and simplify the recommendations generated by the model for the tool users. Some examples of these visualizations might be a real-time park map with the current and predicted occupancy levels, staffing recommendations to optimize employee allocation, and a pricing panel dynamically suggesting optimal ticket prices.

4. **Validating and iterating**

   Lastly, we must ensure that the main users of the tool continuously monitor the accuracy of the model's recommendations, as well as their impact on the park metrics and goals. Some metrics we might want to monitor for validation purposes are: average waiting time per attraction, revenue per visitor, and visitors' satisfaction scores.

6.4 Case Studies

Let's proceed to review a couple of real-world examples of prescriptive analytics implementation; split into optimization and simulation techniques.

Table 6.1	Overview of prescriptive analytics case studies

Optimization Techniques	
United Parcel Service (UPS) is one of the biggest package delivery companies in the world. It benefits from using prescriptive analytics for its route optimization. Through the use of this approach, it analyzes data like traffic conditions and delivery addresses to establish the most efficient routes to use.	Delta Airlines also leverages this framework to optimize their flight schedules. They analyze data on aircrew schedules, passengers demand and airplanes availability to identify the most efficient and profitable flight schedules.

Simulation Techniques	
Procter & Gamble (P&G) teams simulate different supply chain scenarios like disruptions and fluctuations. This enables them to maintain optimal inventory levels at all times, while also guaranteeing on-time delivery.	Disney leverages simulation techniques to build multiple scenarios. For this, it uses attributes such as varying visitors flow, rides occupancy levels and staff availability to predict and efficiently manage their visitors flow through the park, and their day-to-day operations.

Chapter Summary

◆ Prescriptive analytics is an advanced analytics method that predicts future outcomes and suggests actions to achieve desired goals, using techniques like optimization, decision analysis, and scenario simulation.

◆ Optimization techniques include methods such as Linear Programming, Integer Programming, and Nonlinear Programming, which are used to find the best possible outcomes by adjusting certain variables within set constraints.

◆ Simulation techniques comprise methods like Monte Carlo Simulation, Discrete Event Simulation, and Agent-Based Modeling, which help in understanding potential outcomes by modeling different scenarios and analyzing their impacts.

Quiz

1. **What is the primary goal of prescriptive analytics?**
   a. To analyze past data
   b. To predict future outcomes
   c. To suggest actions for achieving desired goals
   d. To visualize data

2. **Which technique in prescriptive analytics involves finding the best possible outcomes by adjusting variables within set constraints?**
   a. Descriptive analytics
   b. Predictive analytics
   c. Optimization techniques
   d. Simulation techniques

3. **What is Linear Programming commonly used for in prescriptive analytics?**
   a. Data visualization
   b. Predicting sales trends
   c. Optimizing resource allocation
   d. Generating random variables

4. **Which of the following is a type of simulation technique?**
   a. Regression analysis
   b. Monte Carlo Simulation
   c. Linear programming
   d. Cluster analysis

5. **In which situation would Integer Programming be most appropriate?**

    a. When variables must be whole numbers

    b. When working with continuous variables

    c. For forecasting sales trends

    d. For visualizing data trends

6. **What does a Monte Carlo Simulation primarily help with?**

    a. Determining the best course of action based on past data

    b. Exploring different scenarios and their outcomes

    c. Predicting future market trends

    d. Analyzing historical data

7. **What is the main difference between Linear and Nonlinear Programming?**

    a. The type of data they use

    b. The constraints and relationships between variables

    c. The complexity of the problem

    d. The type of industries that use them

8. **Why is it important to continuously validate and iterate on prescriptive models?**

    a. To ensure the model remains accurate and effective

    b. To reduce the complexity of the model

    c. To align with historical data trends

    d. To lower the cost of implementation

9. **In the context of BI, what does the implementation of prescriptive analytics often require?**
   a. Simple data collection tools
   b. Basic spreadsheets
   c. Advanced analytics and optimization tools
   d. Historical data analysis

10. **Which is a key benefit of using prescriptive analytics in business decision-making?**
    a. It helps visualize past data
    b. It predicts future trends without suggesting actions
    c. It provides actionable recommendations for optimal decision-making
    d. It simplifies data collection processes

Answers	1 – c	2 – c	3 – c	4 – b	5 – a
	6 – b	7 – b	8 – a	9 – c	10 – c

This page is intentionally left blank

Chapter **7**

Data Visualization in BI

KEY LEARNING OBJECTIVES

- Understand how data visualization complements and enhances the insights gained from the four types of data analytics.
- Learn how to make the right choice of chart types and interactive elements to effectively present your data.
- Explore principles that ensure your visualizations are both engaging and informative, avoiding common pitfalls.

Having understood the four primary types of data analytics, we can now change gears and explore another vital aspect of Business Intelligence: Data Visualization. Through the techniques we have covered in the previous three chapters, we can generate strategic insights. However, it is only by making them visual that we will be able to present them compellingly to our stakeholders. In this chapter, we will explore the power of data visualization to make our insights understandable and accessible.

It is true that this component of the business intelligence framework is often seen as the "fun" side of BI, but the importance of getting this step right cannot be overstated. Effective data visualization can be a deal breaker when proposing recommendations and plans to our leadership team; and I am confident that by the end of this chapter you will understand why.

7.1 Why Data Visualization Matters in BI?

For context, when you get to this point in BI, you have probably already spent a couple of weeks working with numbers, analyzing patterns, and making sense of your data. At this stage, you are probably excited because you will soon be ready to share your work and positively influence your team's decisions.

Previously, you would have probably presented a 10+ page report full of tables and charts that you already knew, did not communicate anything concise, and did not trigger a fruitful discussion. Does this sound familiar? Even if this does not resonate with you, believe me when I say that the described situation takes place day in and day out in boardrooms.

Truth be told, not everyone gets as excited about spreadsheets and numbers as some of us do. However, everyone is impressed by a well-crafted visual that efficiently translates the story told by our data.

Let's break down the specific factors that demonstrate why data visualization is so crucial in BI:

1. **Data visualization connects with our brains**

   It is often said that a picture is worth a thousand words. In reality, our brain actually processes visual information 60,000 times faster than text; taking only 13 milliseconds.[20] Read that again: sixty thousand times faster. In a world where attention spans keep shrinking, enabling quick information processing is invaluable.

---

20. Mary C. Potter, Brad Wyble, Carl Erick Hagmann, and Emily S. McCourt, *"Detecting Meaning in RSVP at 13 ms per Picture,"* *Attention, Perception, & Psychophysics* 76, no. 2 (2014): 270-279.

2. **Data visualization makes data accessible**

From my experience, and perhaps you have witnessed this as well, we generally observe a knowledge gap between the team that crunches numbers and is purely data-driven, and everybody else. Luckily, data visualization comes in handy to bridge that gap. It translates those complex BI insights into a language that everyone can understand. Certainly, the more people who comprehend and engage with our data, the better decisions our teams will be able to make.

3. **Data visualization tells a story**

It is no secret that humans love a good story. We have been telling them and passing them down from generation to generation since the beginning of our times. And this is precisely what effective data visualization allows us to do: engage our audience by telling compelling, data-driven stories. These stories end up resonating and sticking with people long after the meeting has ended. They influence decisions and empower us to drive action.

4. **Data visualization reveals the unknown**

Sometimes, the solution to our problems is so obvious, just lying right in front of us, that we end up overlooking it entirely. I am sure you will understand what I am talking about if you have ever participated in an escape game-room challenge. Similarly, data visualization can reveal insights that otherwise would go unnoticed in a sea of numbers.

7.2 The Cognitive Science Behind Data Visualization in BI

To truly appreciate the power of data visualization in business intelligence, you must understand how our brains process visual information. The effectiveness of data visualization does not lie in just creating pretty pictures. It is deeply rooted in cognitive science and the way our minds work.

- **Visual processing speed**

  As mentioned earlier in this chapter, our brains are wired to process visual information in as quickly as 13 milliseconds.[21] This rapid processing allows us to grasp complex information quickly when presented visually, making data visualization an invaluable tool in the fast-paced world of business decision-making.

- **Pattern identification**

  Humans have an innate ability to identify patterns. Our minds are always seeking out specific patterns and relationships in the data we absorb. Data visualization leverages these natural skills by displaying data in a manner that quickly reveals patterns and trends. This is especially important in BI, where discovering patterns in large datasets can result in accurate action plans and efficient resource allocation.[22]

- **Reducing brain work**

  Let me quickly introduce you to John Sweller's cognitive load theory, where he suggests that our working memory can only hold a certain amount of information.[23] That is the reason why we can feel mentally overloaded when faced with substantial amounts of unprocessed information. Data visualization in the BI framework assists in decreasing cognitive stress by displaying data in a more understandable manner. Rather than attempting to retain several pieces of information in our working memory at

---

21. Potter et al., *"Detecting Meaning in RSVP at 13 ms per Picture."*

22. Colin Ware, *Information Visualization: Perception for Design* (Waltham, MA: Morgan Kaufmann, 2013).

23. John Sweller, "Cognitive Load Theory, Learning Difficulty, and Instructional Design," *Learning and Instruction* 4, no. 4 (1994): 295-312.

once, we can shift some of that cognitive load onto the visual representation.

- **The picture superiority phenomenon**

  Studies have consistently demonstrated that individuals have better recollection of pictures compared to words, a concept named the 'picture superiority effect.'[24] In the BI realm, this means that visual insights are easier to recall and act on than textual insights buried in reports with lots of text.

- **Unconscious processing**

  Our brains process specific visual characteristics like color, size, and shape before we become consciously aware of them. This is referred to as 'preattentive processing.'[25] Efficient data visualizations utilize these attributes to emphasize crucial information, enabling key insights to immediately stand out.

- **Gestalt principles**

  The principles of visual perception in Gestalt theory describe how we typically group visual elements together.[26] These principles—proximity, similarity, and continuity—play a vital role in designing impactful data visualizations. By comprehending and implementing these principles, we can develop visual representations that effectively direct the viewer's focus and aid in comprehension.

---

24. Allan Paivio and Kalman Csapo, "Picture Superiority in Free Recall: Imagery or Dual Coding?"*Cognitive Psychology* 5, no. 2 (1973): 176-206.

25. Christopher G. Healey and James T. Enns, "Attention and Visual Memory in Visualization and Computer Graphics," *IEEE Transactions on Visualization and Computer Graphics* 18, no. 7 (2012): 1170-1188.

26. Kurt Koffka, *Principles of Gestalt Psychology* (New York: Harcourt, Brace and Company, 1935).

● **Narrative and context**

Finally, our brains are inherently designed for narrative. We understand and remember information better when it is presented as part of a comprehensible story.[27] In business intelligence, data visualization can be utilized to narrate a story using data. Such a story offers background and storytelling to aid stakeholders in grasping not only the findings, but also its significance.

By leveraging these cognitive principles, BI professionals can produce data visualizations that are more powerful. They can share information in a way that matches the natural information processing of our brains. This framework of data visualization, based on cognitive science, can result in quicker, more precise understanding and improved decision-making in our organizations.

7.3 Types of Data Visualization and Their Applications

There are different data visualization techniques and applications, which we will explore in this section:

7.3.1 Common chart types and when to use them

In the same way that we have learnt about the science behind how humans process information, there is a certain science to choosing the right type of chart for the data we want to present. Within the world of BI, each chart type serves a specific purpose, and it is crucial that you are familiar with them in order to communicate effectively with your audience.

---

27. Michael F. Dahlstrom, "Using Narratives and Storytelling to Communicate Science with Nonexpert Audiences," *Proceedings of the National Academy of Sciences* 111, no. Supplement 4 (2014): 13614-13620.

1. Bar charts

Very straightforward and versatile, making them one of the key players in BI reporting. They are remarkably good for comparing quantities across multiple categories, while they can also be used to:

- Illustrate rankings for different categories
- Display survey results
- Performance comparison of teams, production lines, etc

Example: You could use a bar chart to illustrate the quantity of sales for various products during the previous month; with each bar representing one product.

2. Line charts

Ideal for showing trends and changes over time. They are excellent for forecasting; other use cases might be:

- Tracking changes over time
- Showing relationships between two variables
- Predicting future trends

Example: Line charts are often used to graphically represent the variations in temperature within a day/week/month/year.

3. Pie charts

While often overused (more on this to come later in the chapter), pie charts can be effective for showing parts of a whole, especially when there are a few categories. When to use pie charts:

- To display proportion or relative sizes of parts to a whole
- To show percentage distribution
- To compare parts of a whole

Example: We could choose a pie chart to represent the size of the market that each company in an industry controls; usually referred to as "market segment share."

4. Scatter plots

Excellent for showing relationships between two variables, and identifying correlations or outliers. Most popular use cases:

- Examining relationships between variables
- Identifying correlations
- Spotting clusters or outliers

Example: A scatter plot could be leveraged to visually represent the existing relationship between our marketing spending and sales revenue achieved, revealing potential trends or outliers in a simple manner.

5. Heat maps

Heat maps, often underestimated, use color-coding to represent different values and are particularly useful for showing patterns in large datasets. When to use:

- Showing patterns in complex datasets
- Visualizing data across multiple dimensions
- Identifying hotspots or trends

Example: Heat maps are frequently used to illustrate website daily traffic intensity, emphasizing time periods where the attention reached its peak.

6. Histogram

Histograms are very similar to bar charts in concept, also featuring a column-based display, but they serve quite a different purpose. While bar charts compare categories, histograms display the frequency of a continuous numerical dataset. This might sound a bit confusing at first, but I am confident the specific use cases and examples provided below will help you grasp the variation. When to use:

- Showing distribution of continuous numerical data
- Identifying central tendency, spread and shape of a dataset
- Detecting outliers and understanding patterns

Example: We would use a histogram to display the distribution of exam scores among students, illustrating the number of students that scored within certain ranges.

7. Bullet graphs

Again, another variation of bar charts, commonly used to show progress towards a specific pre-defined goal or target, in a very compact way. When to use:

- Compare metrics performance against targets
- Track progress against goals
- Monitor Key Performance Indicators (KPIs)

Example: You could use a bullet graph to show employees' sales performance against their personal target.

8. Funnel charts

Funnel charts are ideal for visualizing stages in a process, and showing potential drop-offs between stages.When to use:

- Displaying the different stages in a sales process
- Showing conversion rates through a pipeline
- Visualizing user flow through a website

Example: Use a funnel chart to show how many sales leads progress through each stage of your pipeline.

In below Figure 7.1, you will find a visual illustration of the chart types reviewed in this section.

| Figure 7.1 | An overview of the most popular chart types |

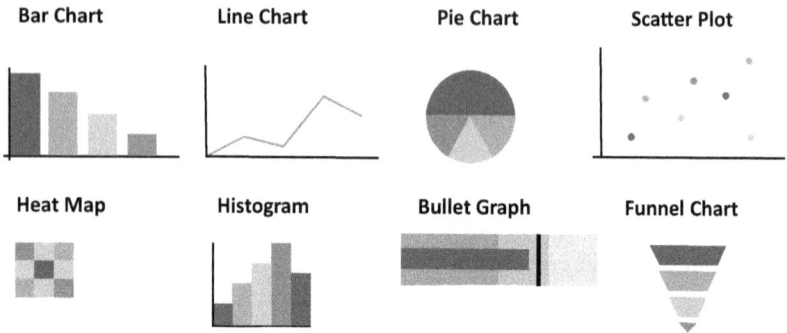

Bar Chart   Line Chart   Pie Chart   Scatter Plot

Heat Map   Histogram   Bullet Graph   Funnel Chart

Choosing the right chart type is as much an art as it is a science. Consider your data, your audience, and the story you want to tell. Remember, the goal in BI is not just to display data, but to communicate insights effectively. Sometimes, combining multiple chart types or using interactive elements can provide a more comprehensive view of your data.

In the next section, we will explore how to bring these various chart types together into cohesive dashboards. This will provide you with a more holistic view of your business data.

7.3.2 Dashboards: Putting it all together

Alright, let's do a quick recap because this chapter is packed with nuggets of impactful takeaways. So far, you have learned about the science behind how our human brains process information, and the art of choosing the right chart type for each occasion. Now, it is time to move into the superstar of Business Intelligence: "Dashboards," where the above individual charts come together to help us tell our story. Since we already looked at how to build a BI report in Chapter Four (see section 4.3.2), now we can concentrate on three other angles:

1. Why do dashboards matter in BI?

- **The big picture:** Dashboards provide both the big picture and the finer details. You get an overview of your business health without losing access to the details.

- **Time-saver:** Instead of digging through multiple reports, you get all your crucial information in one spot; at a glance.

- **Continuous synchronization:** As we learned in Chapter Three, many modern BI tools have the functionality to leverage real-time data, ensuring we are always looking at the latest information available.

- **Customization:** Different audiences need different data, and dashboards allow us to meet this requirement, by empowering us to adjust our solution to each occasion.

2. What should you be careful with?

- **Data overload:** More is not always better, but this is frequently forgotten. The ideal dashboard should simplify the processing of information for our audience. More on this to come in section 7.3.

- **Mismatched metrics:** Make sure the data you are showing actually relates to one another. This might sound super obvious but can be easily forgotten. Putting your coffee shop's daily special next to your quarterly earnings does not make sense.

- **Ignoring context:** Numbers in a vacuum are meaningless. Make sure your dashboard provides context for the metrics it is showing.

- **Poor performance:** Quite a straightforward one, but a slow dashboard will just not be used. It will be very tough to convince our stakeholders to adopt a BI solution that takes 10 minutes to load. Ensure your dashboard loads quickly and updates smoothly.

3. What does a real dashboard look like?

Consider the following parameters:

- A line chart showing your daily sales trends
- A bar chart that compares the performance of each product family
- A heat map displaying sales by region
- A funnel chart that displays the conversion rates
- Some key metrics like total revenue, average order value, and customer acquisition cost

You are rightly thinking that the above sounds too simple, but that is exactly what we should aim for, simplifying information processing. With that, we should be able to spot trends and identify top performers and areas that might need improvement or further exploration, all in one place.

7.4 Principles of Effective Data Visualization

Before we close this chapter, I also wanted to share with you some of the most popular principles for enhancing your data visualization techniques. While they may sound fairly straightforward, it is crucial that you don't overlook them.

7.4.1 Less is more

As introduced in section 7.1, this concept has become highly relevant today. The "data-ink ratio" is a concept introduced by Edward Tufte, a pioneer in data visualization. He argues that we should maximize the data-ink ratio, which means using a minimum amount of visual elements to display the maximum amount of data.[28] In essence, if an element does not add value, it is likely just clutter; so do not be precious about it and just remove it.

---

28. Edward R. Tufte, *The Visual Display of Quantitative Information*, 2nd ed. (Cheshire, CT: Graphics Press, 2001), 93.

Curious about how to implement this? Let's explore it together:

- **Forget the fancy:** This might surprise you but 3D effects, gradients, and elaborate backgrounds more often than not, don't contribute to data understanding. They usually just distract from the core message you are trying to convey.

- **Embrace white spaces:** Do not think of empty space as wasted. It enables a more relaxed digestion of your reporting, making the data easier to process and understand.

- **Simplify scales:** Consider whether every tick mark on an axis is necessary. Simple, standardized scales can make data easier to process at a glance.

- **Make it pop:** Even if we focus on sharing only relevant content on our dashboard, not all data will carry the same weight. The key is to emphasize the most important information and allow secondary data to recede into the background.

Always remember the goal is not to share all the work and volumes of data you have compiled throughout this process, but rather to communicate key insights clearly and effectively. A famous quote that always comes in handy here, and that I would like you to remember, by the wise Leonardo da Vinci: "Simplicity is the ultimate sophistication."[29]

7.4.2 Context, color, and storytelling

In this section, I want us to dive into the art of three vital components: context, color and storytelling. Let's explore how they can help us when it comes to data visualization in BI.

1. **Context**

   We can think of context as the background story that gives meaning to our data. Without it, data points can be perceived as isolated facts that do not tell the complete

---

29. This quote is often attributed to Leonardo da Vinci, though its exact origin is disputed.

story. Therefore, this component is key to ensure our audience understands not just the "what" but the "why" behind our numbers.

- **Clear labels and titles:** We want users to easily understand what is being presented. Clear, concise labels and titles will steer how users consume our reporting.

- **Strategic annotations:** Highlight key points or explain anomalies directly on your visualization, which help drive users' attention to the most important items.

- **Relevant benchmarks:** Numbers often gain meaning through comparison. By providing relevant benchmark guidelines such as year-over-year or industry standards, we can help our users understand the significance of our data.

2. Color

More than an aesthetic treat, color is indeed a powerful tool for communication; although it needs to be used carefully. Let's look at some frequent guidelines for its utilization:

- **Giving it purpose:** Each color should serve a specific function, whether it is highlighting important data, grouping related information, or showing progression.

- **Making it accessible:** Be mindful of color blindness, which affects approximately 8% of men and 0.5% of women.[30] A recommended procedure to support those with visual impairments is to use high-contrast color combinations.

- **Embracing chromatic psychology:** As you have likely heard before, colors can induce specific emotional responses such as red for negative performance and green for growth. Additionally, these associations and interpretations can vary considerably across different

---

30. Jenny M. Birch, "Worldwide Prevalence of Red-Green Color Deficiency," *Journal of the Optical Society of America A* 29, no. 3 (2012): 313-320.

cultures, which I would highly recommend being mindful of; especially if you work with cross-regional teams.[31]

3. Storytelling

Storytelling in data visualization is our ultimate ally to ensure we help our audience understand the bigger picture. Find below frequent storytelling guidelines from a BI perspective:

- **Clear central message:** Identify the main point you want to convey, and let this guide every aspect of your visualization.

- **Logical design:** Just as it happens with every good story, we will want our data to follow a clear structure; with a clear start (context), middle (insights), and end (call to action).

- **Relevant visual choices:** Select chart types and design elements that best support your narrative. As covered in section 7.3, each chart type serves a specific purpose, so we need to pick them wisely.

- **Audience engagement:** When appropriate, use interactive elements to enable your audience to explore the data themselves. This can lead to deeper engagement and understanding.

By sticking to these principles of simplicity, you will create visualizations and reporting that inspire and motivate your audience to take action.

---

31. Satyendra Singh, "Impact of Color on Marketing," *Management Decision* 44, no. 6 (2006): 783-789.

7.5 Common Pitfalls and How to Avoid Them

While we are on the subject of principles for effective data visualization, it is also a good time to go through common data visualization mistakes and how to proactively avoid them. To illustrate the point, I will also include a very simple example for each of these pitfalls:

1. **Choosing the wrong chart**

   An incorrect choice of charts is one of the most common mistakes in data visualization, which can confuse your audience.

   How to avoid: Always consider the nature and purpose of your data. What do you want to communicate?
   A very good resource I would like to share here with you is Stephen Few's "Graph Selection Matrix,"[32] an excellent cheat sheet when selecting chart types. You can also refer to section 7.3 on "Types of Data Visualizations and Their Applications" to evaluate various chart types and choose the right chart from a BI perspective, based on your requirements.

---

32. Stephen Few, *Show Me the Numbers: Designing Tables and Graphs to Enlighten*, 2nd ed. (Burlingame, CA: Analytics Press, 2012), 59-70.

| Figure 7.2 | An illustration of choosing the wrong chart |

Wrong choice: Very hard to compare values

Correct choice: Easier to compare values

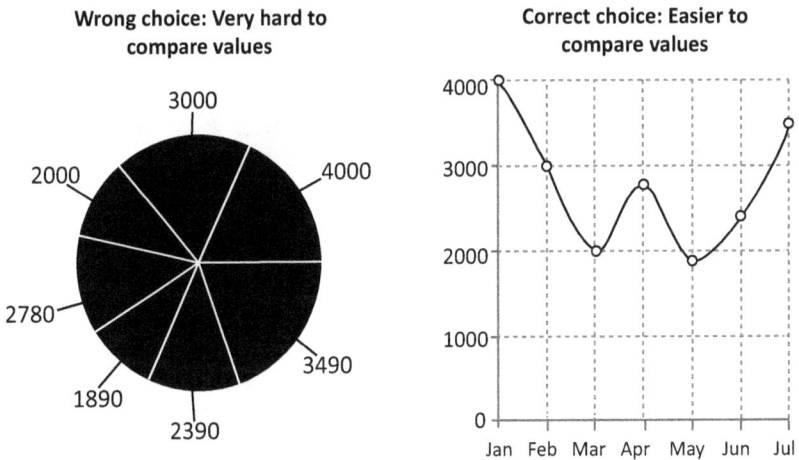

2. Misleading scales

Manipulating scales, intentionally or not, can dramatically alter the perception of your data. A very typical example is using a non-zero baseline for bar charts, which can exaggerate differences between values.

How to avoid: Always start your y-axis at zero for bar charts. For line charts, choose a scale that provides context without distorting the data. If you must deviate from this guideline, be transparent with your audience.

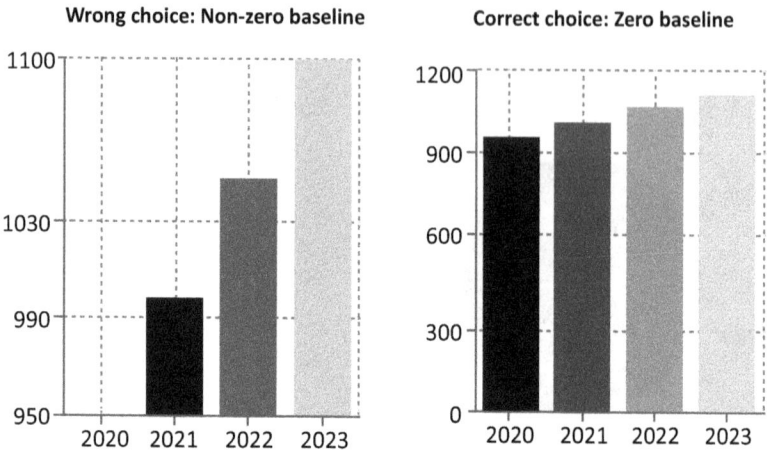

Figure 7.3 An illustration of misleading scales

3. Overcomplicating visualizations

Remember you do not need to show all the work and data you have been compiling while working on this BI framework.

How to avoid: Embrace the principle of data-ink ratio as we discussed earlier. Focus on the key message and remove any elements that don't contribute to it. You may consider breaking complex visualizations into multiple, simpler charts if necessary.

| Figure 7.4 | An illustration of overcomplicating visualizations |

Wrong choice: Overcomplicated chart   Correct choice: Simplified chart

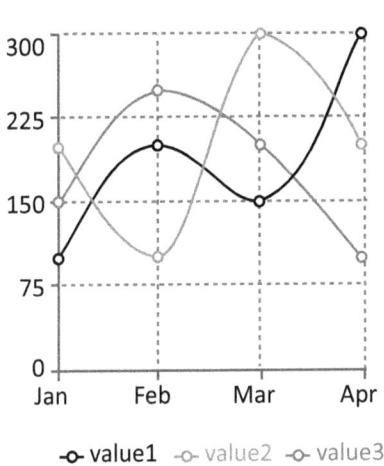

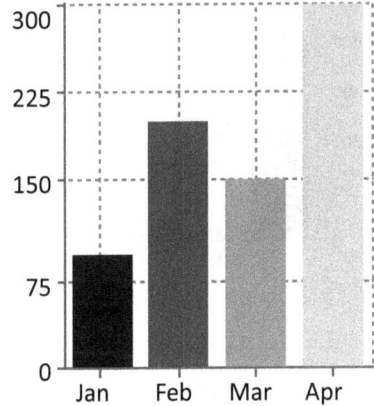

-o- value1 -o- value2 -o- value3

4. Ignoring accessibility

Failing to consider color-blind individuals or those with other visual impairments can exclude a significant portion of your audience.

How to avoid: Use color-blind-friendly palettes, ensure sufficient contrast, and consider using patterns or labels in addition to color to convey information. Tools like the Coblis Color Blindness Simulator[33] can help you test your visualizations.

---

33. Coblis - Color Blindness Simulator, Colblindor, Retrieved from: https://www.color-blindness.com

Figure 7.5   **An illustration of ignoring accessibility**

Wrong choice: Not colorblind friendly   Correct choice: Colorblind friendly

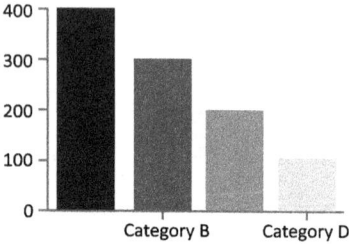

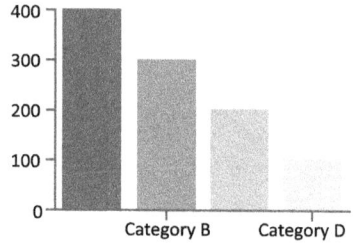

5. **Misusing 3D effects**

While 3D charts might seem visually appealing, they often distort data and make it harder to compare values accurately.

How to avoid: In most cases, stick to 2D representations. If you must use 3D, ensure it serves a purpose, such as in scientific or medical imaging, and does not compromise data integrity.

Figure 7.6   **An illustration of misusing 3D effects**

Wrong choice: Irrelevant 3D effect   Correct choice: Simple 2D chart

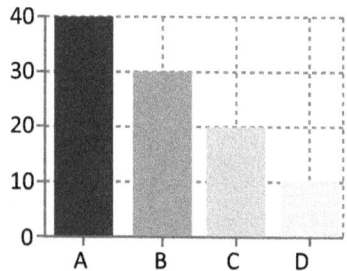

6. Neglecting to provide context

Presenting data without proper context can lead to misinterpretation or failure to convey the significance of your insights.

How to avoid: Always provide relevant context, such as time periods, data sources, and any assumptions or limitations. Use annotations to highlight key points or explain anomalies.

Figure 7.7 **An illustration of neglecting to provide context**

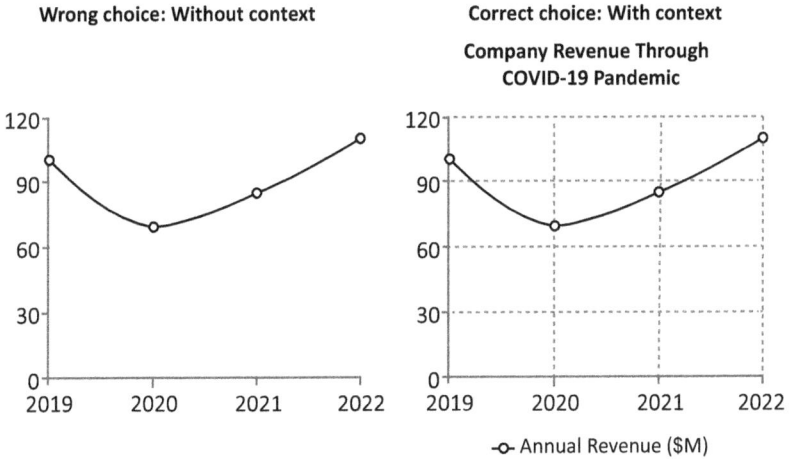

Wrong choice: Without context

Correct choice: With context

Company Revenue Through COVID-19 Pandemic

-o- Annual Revenue ($M)

7. Inconsistent design elements

Inconsistencies in color schemes, fonts, or styles across different charts can make your visualizations look unprofessional and harder to interpret.

How to avoid: Develop and adhere to a consistent style guide for your visualizations. This includes color schemes, font choices, and overall design elements.

Figure 7.8 An illustration of inconsistent design elements

Wrong choice: Inconsistent design   Correct choice: Consistent design

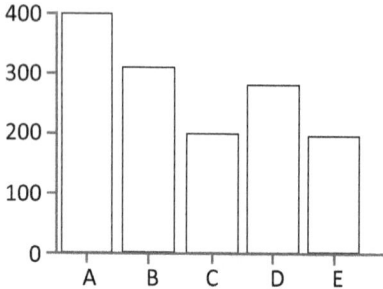

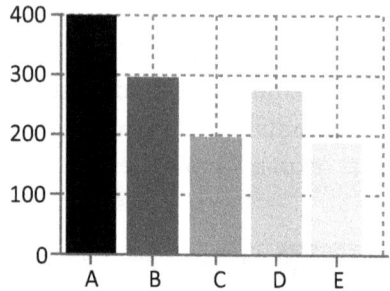

8. Prioritizing aesthetics over clarity

While visually appealing charts can capture attention, prioritizing aesthetics at the expense of clarity can undermine the effectiveness of your visualization.

How to avoid: Always prioritize clarity and accuracy. Use design elements to enhance understanding, not just for decorative purposes. Remember, the primary goal is to communicate information effectively.

Figure 7.9 An illustration of prioritizing aesthetics over clarity

Wrong choice: Pretty but unclear   Correct choice: Clear and informative

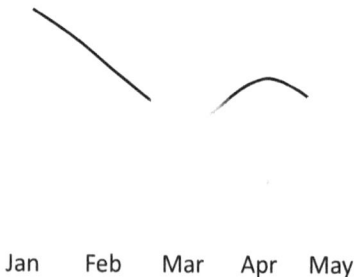

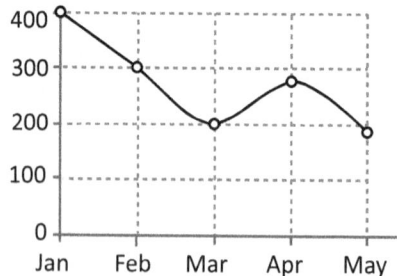

By being aware of these common pitfalls and actively working to avoid them, you can significantly improve the quality and effectiveness of your data visualizations. Remember, the goal is to create visually appealing charts and communicate insights clearly and accurately, enabling your audience to make informed decisions.

Chapter Summary

◆ We studied the crucial role of data visualization in making insights understandable and actionable. By leveraging visual aids, we can communicate complex data efficiently, making it accessible to a broader audience.

◆ The way our brains process visual information helps in designing effective data visualizations. Concepts like pattern recognition, the picture superiority effect, and preattentive processing highlight how visuals can simplify complex data.

◆ Each chart type across bar charts, line charts, pie charts, scatter plots, heat maps, histograms, bullet graphs, and funnel charts, serves a specific purpose and is best suited for particular data representation needs.

◆ A dashboard is a powerful tool for presenting a cohesive view of business data, allowing for real-time monitoring and decision-making. It is essential to understand the importance of customization, avoiding data overload, and ensuring relevant metrics are used.

◆ Principles such as "less is more," appropriate use of context and color, and the art of storytelling, ensure that data visualizations are not only informative but also engaging and easy to understand.

◆ Understanding common mistakes in data visualization and strategies to avoid these pitfalls helps enhance the clarity and effectiveness of visualizations.

Quiz

1. **What is the primary purpose of data visualization in Business Intelligence (BI)?**
   a. To collect data
   b. To make data understandable and actionable
   c. To store data securely
   d. To eliminate data redundancy

2. **Why are visuals processed faster by our brains compared to text?**
   a. Visuals are more colorful
   b. Visuals are simpler
   c. Our brains are wired to process visual information quickly
   d. Text requires translation into visual images

3. **Which cognitive principle helps in recognizing patterns in data visualization?**
   a. Cognitive Load Theory
   b. Picture Superiority Effect
   c. Preattentive Processing
   d. Pattern Recognition

4. **What is a key benefit of using bar charts in BI reporting?**
   a. They can show complex statistical relationships
   b. They are effective for comparing quantities across categories
   c. They provide detailed narrative explanations
   d. They are suitable for displaying continuous data distributions

5. **When should a pie chart be used in data visualization?**

   a. To compare trends over time

   b. To show parts of a whole

   c. To display hierarchical data

   d. To illustrate complex relationships

6. **What is a scatter plot primarily used for in data visualization?**

   a. Comparing sales figures

   b. Displaying time series data

   c. Examining relationships between two variables

   d. Showing parts of a whole

7. **How does a heat map typically display data?**

   a. Using color coding to represent values

   b. Using lines to show trends

   c. Using bars to compare categories

   d. Using pie slices to show proportions

8. **What is the purpose of a funnel chart in data visualization?**

   a. To compare historical data

   b. To visualize stages in a process

   c. To represent frequency distributions

   d. To display real-time data updates

9. **According to Edward Tufte, what should be maximized in data visualization?**

   a. The complexity of visual elements

   b. The data-ink ratio

   c. The use of 3D effects

   d. The number of data points displayed

10. **Why is it important to consider accessibility in data visualization?**

   a. To make visuals more colorful

   b. To ensure all users, including those with visual impairments, can understand the data

   c. To make the visuals more detailed

   d. To increase the complexity of the data presentation

Answers	1 – b	2 – c	3 – d	4 – b	5 – b
	6 – c	7 – a	8 – b	9 – b	10 – b

This page is intentionally left blank

Chapter 8

Implementing and Maintaining BI Systems

KEY LEARNING OBJECTIVES

- Understand components of BI project management and implementation strategies.
- Learn how to manage organizational change and foster user adoption of new BI systems.
- Identify common implementation challenges and explore best practices to overcome them.
- Recognize the importance of effective maintenance and continuous improvement in BI systems.

Having covered all the key components of BI systems, for the last part of the book I would like us to concentrate on their actual implementation and management—another crucial element to guarantee a successful adoption.

Hence, through this chapter we will explore multiple techniques to bring our BI system to life and overcome any challenges we might encounter during its implementation.

8.1 BI Project Management and Implementation Strategies

Bringing all the previous BI components together and implementing a successful BI system requires a very structured approach, which I will break down below into three critical elements.

8.1.1 The crucial role of project management

A non-negotiable foundation to guarantee the successful implementation of BI is solid project management. Interestingly though, traditional approaches are becoming obsolete when it comes to BI, due to its fast-paced, ever-changing nature. This is why more modern frameworks like "Agile" have gained a lot of traction recently in the BI world. But what is Agile?

As author Ken Collier clearly defines in his book,[34] "Agile is the approach to software development, under which requirements and solutions evolve through the collaborative effort of self-organizing and cross-functional teams and their customer(s)/ end user(s)."

After reading that definition and recalling our learnings so far in this book, you probably understand why the Agile framework has become so tightly linked to business intelligence. In that brief definition, we can already spot three important factors that align perfectly with our BI requirements:

- **Adaptability:** Since BI requirements will constantly be changing as the project progresses, an Agile approach will allow you to pivot quickly without impacting the rhythm and progress of the entire project.

---

34. Ken Collier, *Agile Analytics: A Value-Driven Approach to Business Intelligence and Data Warehousing* (Boston: Addison-Wesley Professional, 2011), 121.

- **Incremental delivery:** This methodology enables teams to concentrate on producing smaller and more manageable deliverables every few weeks for our stakeholders, without requiring us to have a final solution completed in order to move forward.

- **Stakeholder involvement:** As called out in the definition, "collaborative effort," regular cooperation and alignment are the keys to success when it comes to BI.

Remember though, Agile is not a magic wand. It will require commitment and a shift in mindset from traditional project management approaches. But when done right, it can be a game-changer for your BI implementation.

8.1.2 Crafting your implementation strategy

With our project management approach in place, let's talk "strategy." You should think of the BI implementation strategy as your game plan – it outlines how you will get from "point A," your current business state, to "point B," your shiny new BI system.

Here are some key elements to consider:

- **Phased rollout:** Do not try to boil the ocean. Start with a pilot project or a single department before expanding. This approach, often called the "crawl-walk-run" strategy, allows you to figure out complications and build momentum.[35]

- **Data governance:** Do you remember the emphasis on (high) data quality that we discussed in earlier chapters? Well, time to put it into practice! Establish clear data governance policies from the get-go. Trust me, future-you will thank present-you for this. We will delve deeper into data governance in Chapter Nine.

---

35. William Yeoh and Andy Koronios, "Critical Success Factors for Business Intelligence Systems," *Journal of Computer Information Systems* 50, no. 3 (2010): 23-32.

- **Training and support:** Your BI system is only as good as the people using it. Invest in comprehensive training programs and ongoing support. Ensure not to rush it or make it a one-and-done deal. Learning to use BI tools effectively is an ongoing process.

- **Performance metrics:** How will you know if your BI implementation is successful? Define clear, measurable KPIs before you start. These could include user adoption rates, time saved in report generation, or improvements in decision-making speed.

- **Feedback loop:** Create channels for users to provide feedback. This is not just about being nice, user feedback is gold dust for continuous improvement.

Let me share a quick anecdote that illustrates why a well-planned, phased rollout matters when it comes to implementing BI effectively. A few years back, I was supporting a company with their BI implementation. They were all very keen on rolling out the system company-wide in one big bang. Despite my reservations, they pushed ahead. The result? A spectacular flop. Users were overwhelmed, data quality issues cropped up frequently, and the project nearly got scrapped entirely.

Luckily, we were able to course-correct. We scaled back, focused on a pilot with the supply chain department, and took a phased approach. It took longer than originally planned, but the result was a robust BI system that got used and delivered real value.

The moral of the story? In BI implementation, slow and steady often wins the race.

8.1.3 Building your dream team

Of course, I cannot finish this implementation section without talking about people; an element so crucial that will have the power to either make or break your project implementation. The ideal mix of skills you should be looking for will cover everything from technical wizards who can handle your data and business-savvy folks who can grasp strategic implications, to change management experts who can support you through the transition period seamlessly.

Here is a quick rundown of key roles you will want to consider:

- **BI project manager:** Your conductor, keeping all the moving parts in harmony.
- **Data architects:** The professionals who design your data infrastructure.
- **Extract, Transform, Load (ETL) developers:** These are your data plumbers, making sure data flows smoothly from source to destination.
- **BI developers:** The magicians who turn raw data into insightful reports and dashboards.
- **Business analysts:** Your translators between tech-speak and business needs.
- **Change management specialist:** Do not underestimate this role as they will be crucial in driving user adoption.

Remember, these roles are not necessarily one-to-one with individuals. In smaller organizations, you might have people wearing multiple hats. The key is ensuring all these bases are covered.[36]

Implementing a BI system is no small feat. It requires careful planning, the right approach, and an outstanding team. But get it right and you will be amazed at the transformation it can bring to your organization's decision-making capabilities.

---

36. Mohamed Z. Elbashir, Peter A. Collier, and Michael J. Davern, "Measuring the Effects of Business Intelligence Systems: The Relationship between Business Process and Organizational Performance," *International Journal of Accounting Information Systems* 9, no. 3 (2008): 135-153.

8.2 Change Management and User Adoption

These two aspects will be fundamental to ensure a successful BI implementation, which is why I decided they deserve their own section in this chapter. Here, we will go through these topics and examine them from three different perspectives. I have included relevant statistics and quotes where applicable, to better showcase their importance:

8.2.1 The human side

Apart from the obvious technical difficulty, implementing a BI system is also a people challenge. As John Kotter, the guru of change management, described in his book,[37] "The central issue is never strategy, structure, culture, or systems. The core of the matter is always about changing the behavior of people." And this could not be more accurate.

Keep in mind that throughout this BI process, you are asking people to i) use a new tool; ii) change how they work and how they make decisions; and iii) reevaluate what they think about their role in the organization. That is no small ask.

Let's see how we can approach this challenge in the next sections.

8.2.2 The change management process

While there is no one-size-fits-all approach to tackle this phase of the project, there are multiple techniques that can assist us here, as explained below:

- **Creating urgency:** From the very beginning of this project, you should work on convincing your team about why implementing this BI system is crucial for the organization's success. As Kotter explains, "People will

---

37. John P. Kotter, *Leading Change* (Boston: Harvard Business School Press, 1996).

find a thousand ingenious ways to withhold cooperation from a process they don't understand."[38]

- **Building a guiding coalition:** You need champions at all levels of the organization. These are your cheerleaders, your early adopters, the folks who will help spread the gospel of BI. One of the most common reasons for BI project failure is the lack of involvement from leadership;[39] so get those leaders on board first!

- **Developing a clear vision:** The sooner you can create a robust vision and share this with your colleagues, the more you will guarantee yourself a smooth implementation and adoption later on.

- **Communicating, communicating, communicating:** When you think you have communicated enough, communicate some more. Is it clear yet? Use every single channel at your disposal - weekly business reviews, newsletters, intranets, and even good old-fashioned coffee break conversations. As change management expert Prosci notes in their research, "Projects with excellent change management are six times more likely to meet objectives than those with poor change management."[40]

- **Removing obstacles:** Throughout the entire BI system implementation, I would highly recommend you always keep an eye on whatever friction you might encounter and tackle it head-on. Is it a lack of training? Old processes that conflict with the new system? Whatever it may be, try to address it and get it out of your way.

- **Creating short-term wins:** Nothing breeds success like success. Did someone use the new BI tool to make a decision that saved the company money? Celebrate early victories, no matter how small; let everyone hear about it and join the hype.

---

38. Kotter, *Leading Change.*

39. Stafiz, "The 10 Main Causes of Project Failure," retrieved from https://stafiz.com

40. Prosci, *Best Practices in Change Management,* Prosci Benchmark Report (Loveland, CO: Prosci Inc., 2018).

- **Building on the change:** Talking of hype, utilize the momentum from those early triumphs to drive deeper change. As your team gets more comfortable with the BI system, start pushing the boundaries of what it can do.

- **Embedding change into the culture:** Convince and empower colleagues to integrate BI solutions into their day-to-day activities through performance reviews, decision-making, and strategic reporting processes. There is no excuse to stay out of this wave.

8.2.3 Fostering user adoption

Now, let's zoom in on user adoption. Your fancy BI system will only be as good as the people using it. Thus, let's take a look at some approaches to bring your team on board:

- **Training, and more training:** The same logic that we applied earlier to communication, can now be applied here. There is no just one-and-done training model. Ideally, you will need to pursue ongoing, role-specific training that evolves as your BI system does. As the ancient proverb goes, "Give a man a fish, and you feed him for a day. Teach a man to fish, and you feed him for a lifetime."[41]

- **Discussing shared purpose:** As much as it is feasible for you, spend time showing each team how the BI system can be applied to improve their roles. As change management expert William Bridges puts it, "People don't resist change. They resist loss."[42] Let each team learn about the huge potential of BI adoption.

- **Gamification:** Who says learning can't be fun? Use leaderboards, badges, or even friendly competitions to

---

41. Common proverb of uncertain origin.

42. William Bridges, *Managing Transitions: Making the Most of Change*, 3rd ed. (Philadelphia, PA: Da Capo Press, 2009).

encourage system use. A study by TalentLMS[43] found that 89% of employees believe gamification makes them more productive at work.

- **Creating a support team:** Naturally, some colleagues might need time to get used to the new ways. Ensure you are supportive; set up a help desk or designated office hours for this purpose, appoint BI champions in each department, and create user forums. Essentially, you want to give your team multiple avenues to get help when needed.

- **Leading by example:** If the leadership is not using the BI system, why should anyone else? Get your executives on board to use the system regularly. Nothing drives adoption quite like seeing the boss pull up a dashboard in a meeting.

- **Exchanging regular feedback:** Remember, adoption is not just a single, one-time event, it is a continuous journey. Thus, remember to check in with your users frequently. What is working? What is not? Use this feedback to improve your system and your adoption strategies continually.

I am not going to downplay this. Change management and user adoption are and will be tough. But I can assure you that when it clicks, when your team starts embracing data-driven decision-making, and when you see that light bulb moment as someone leverages insights from your BI tool... Well, that is when the magic happens.

Just one more final remark before closing this section. As Peter Drucker, the father of modern management wisely said, "Culture eats strategy for breakfast."[44] So yes, ensure you get your strategy right, but always remember to bring your people along for the ride. After all, they are the ones who will turn your BI vision into reality.

---

43. TalentLMS, "The 2019 Gamification at Work Survey," retrieved from https://www.talentlms.com
44. Peter F. Drucker, *The Practice of Management* (New York: HarperBusiness, 1993).

8.3 Challenges and Best Practices in BI Implementation

We are almost done with the BI system implementation topic, but before we close the chapter let's walk through some of the common challenges you might face and the best practices to overcome them.

8.3.1 Common challenges in BI implementation

- **Data quality issues:** A survey by Gartner reveals that poor data quality is a primary reason for up to 40% of all business initiatives failing to achieve their targeted benefits.[45] This is indeed why I have been so persistent about ensuring data quality in BI throughout this book.

- **Lack of strategic alignment:** Sadly, more often than not, we see BI/tech teams getting so deeply immersed in the development and implementation work that they end up losing sight and connection with the original business goals. This results in a very impressive-looking tool that does not align with the company and/or team objectives.

- **Resistance to change:** We discussed this in section 8.2, but let's look at the statistics in more detail. A McKinsey study uncovered that 70% of change initiatives do not fulfill their goals, mainly because of employee resistance and lack of leadership support;[46] that is practically 3 out of every 4 initiatives!

- **Scalability issues:** Adapting your BI system simultaneously as your business and data volumes grow can be a challenging task. When researching this topic, Transforming Data With Intelligence (TDWI) found that

---

45. Gartner, "How to Create a Business Case for Data Quality Improvement," retrieved from https://www.gartner.com

46. Scott Keller and Colin Aiken, "The Inconvenient Truth About Change Management," McKinsey & Company, 2009.

4 in 10 organizations mentioned scalability as a major challenge in their BI implementations.[47]

- **Security concerns:** A study published by Verizon shows that 61% of data breaches involved issues with credentials.[48] With great data comes great responsibility, and the need to implement strong security measures; a stage of our project we should not overlook.

8.3.2 Best practices for successful BI implementation

Now that we have looked at the challenges, let's talk about how to overcome them. Here are some best practices that can help you navigate your BI implementation journey smoothly:

- **Starting with a clear strategy:** Before even considering choosing a BI tool, it is key to understand what we want to achieve with the project. Define your objectives, identify your key stakeholders, and align your BI strategy with overall business goals.

- **Prioritizing data quality:** According to a report by Experian, organizations estimate that 29% of their data is inaccurate.[49] That's nearly one-third of one's data. Therefore, from the very beginning, you must invest in data cleansing and data governance processes. You can begin by implementing data quality checks and establishing data stewardship roles. Ensure data quality by making it a continuous and recurring process.

- **Adopting Agile:** As discussed in section 8.1, Agile is also particularly relevant here. This approach will allow you and your team to deliver value incrementally. It will enable you to get feedback early and adjust your progress as needed. A study by the Project Management Institute

---

47. Philip Russom, *Overcoming Obstacles to Data Modernization,* TDWI Best Practices Report (2016).

48. Verizon, *2021 Data Breach Investigations Report* (Verizon, 2021).

49. Experian, *2019 Global Data Management Research* (Experian Information Solutions, Inc., 2019).

found that Agile projects are 28% more successful than traditional projects.[50]

- **Investing in user training and support:** Do not underestimate the importance of training. A study by Brandon Hall Group found that companies that invest in comprehensive training programs have 218% higher revenue per employee.[51] Provide ongoing training, create user guides and Frequently Asked Questions (FAQs), and establish a support system to help users as they navigate the new BI landscape.

- **Choosing the right tools:** This might seem obvious, but it is a crucial step. Your BI tool should align with your business needs. It should be scalable and user-friendly. According to Gartner, in 2025, 80% of organizations seeking to scale digital business will fail because they do not take a modern approach to data and analytics governance.[52] So, choose wisely!

- **Ensuring executive sponsorship:** Having robust executive support can make or break your BI implementation. A study by Prosci found that projects with excellent leadership support are 3.5 times more likely to meet or exceed objectives.[53] Get your C-suite on board, and work on keeping them engaged throughout the process.

- **Focusing on user adoption:** The adoption rate you achieve for your BI system will play a critical role in its success. Make your BI tools intuitive and valuable to users. According to a report by Logi Analytics, 67% of employees

---

50. Project Management Institute, *Pulse of the Profession: Capturing the Value of Project Management* (PMI, 2015).

51. Brandon Hall Group, *Learning Strategy Research Study* (Brandon Hall Group, 2017).

52. Gartner, "Gartner Top 10 Trends in Data and Analytics for 2020," retrieved from https://www.gartner.com

53. Prosci, *Best Practices in Change Management*, Prosci Benchmark Report (Loveland, CO: Prosci Inc., 2018).

say they would use analytics tools more if they were embedded in their daily workflows.[54]

- **Planning for scalability:** Your BI system should be able to grow with your business. This means handling increased data volumes and adapting to new types of data. It also means effectively handling new business questions and new user requirements. As discussed in Chapter Two, leveraging cloud-based BI solutions can offer significant advantages in terms of scalability.

- **Prioritizing security:** Implement robust security measures including data encryption, user authentication, and access controls. We will discuss more on this in Chapter Nine. Regularly audit your security practices and stay up-to-date with the latest security threats and solutions.

- **Measuring and iterating:** Finally, do not assume your work is done once the system is live. Measure regularly the performance and impact of your BI system. Are you meeting the objectives you set out at the start? Are users getting value from the system? You can and should leverage these insights to continuously improve and evolve your BI implementation.

Implementing a BI system is a journey, not a destination; a marathon, not a sprint—whichever resonates more with you. With meticulous planning, strong leadership, and a willingness to adapt and learn continuously, you will be rewarded with insights that can transform your business decision-making.

---

54. Logi Analytics, *2018 State of Embedded Analytics Report* (Logi Analytics, 2018).

Chapter Summary

◆ Project management, especially Agile methodologies, plays a key role in effective BI system implementation.

◆ Practices like phased rollout, data governance, training, performance metrics, and feedback loops must be adhered to ensure seamless implementation.

◆ The ideal structure of a BI project team includes essential roles such as BI project managers, data architects, ETL developers, BI developers, business analysts, and change management specialists.

◆ It is vital to address the human side of BI implementation while fostering a culture of change and ensuring continuous communication and training.

◆ Common challenges in BI implementation include data quality issues, lack of strategic alignment, resistance to change, scalability concerns, and security risks.

◆ Strategies to overcome these challenges include starting with a clear strategy, prioritizing data quality, adopting Agile, investing in user training and support, choosing the right tools, ensuring executive sponsorship, focusing on user adoption, planning for scalability, prioritizing security, and measuring and iterating.

Quiz

1. **What is the primary focus of project management in BI system implementation?**

   a. Data storage

   b. Data visualization

   c. Effective planning and execution

   d. Data cleaning

2. **Which methodology is often preferred for BI system implementation?**

   a. Waterfall

   b. Agile

   c. Lean

   d. Six Sigma

3. **What is the role of a BI project manager?**

   a. Developing data warehouses

   b. Managing project timelines and resources

   c. Cleaning and preparing data

   d. Designing dashboards

4. **Why is data governance important in BI implementation?**

   a. To increase data volume

   b. To ensure data quality and compliance

   c. To decrease data storage costs

   d. To create data visualizations

5. **Which of the following is NOT an essential role in a BI implementation team?**

   a. Data Architect

   b. ETL Developer

   c. Graphic Designer

   d. BI Developer

6. **What is a key strategy for fostering a culture of change during BI implementation?**

   a. Ignoring user feedback

   b. Providing continuous training

   c. Limiting communication

   d. Delaying updates

7. **What is a common challenge in BI implementation?**

   a. Excessive data quality

   b. Lack of strategic alignment

   c. Too much executive sponsorship

   d. Over-training users

8. **How can data quality issues be addressed in BI implementation?**

   a. By ignoring them

   b. By adopting an Agile approach

   c. By ensuring executive sponsorship

   d. By starting with a clear data strategy

9. **Why is it important to have executive sponsorship for BI projects?**
   a. To reduce project costs
   b. To ensure the project has high visibility and support
   c. To avoid data governance issues
   d. To simplify data visualization

10. **What approach can help in overcoming resistance to change?**
   a. Limiting user adoption
   b. Providing minimal training
   c. Ensuring continuous communication and involvement
   d. Ignoring user concerns

Answers	1 – c	2 – b	3 – b	4 – b	5 – c
	6 – b	7 – b	8 – d	9 – b	10 – c

This page is intentionally left blank

Chapter **9**

Data Management in BI

KEY LEARNING OBJECTIVES

- Recognize the importance of data governance in BI systems and learn key strategies for implementation.

- Explore methods for ensuring and maintaining data quality throughout the BI lifecycle.

- Understand the critical role of data security and privacy in BI operations.

- Learn best practices for protecting sensitive information while maximizing the value of your data.

Before we part ways, I still have two powerful chapters reserved for you. Since you are now familiar with the process and complexities of implementing a BI system, I want to ensure that you are set up for long-term success. Thus, we must look in more detail at how to efficiently and safely manage our data, a critical component of this process.

9.1 Data Governance and Quality Management

First things first. Let's kick things off with data governance and quality management—two sides of the same coin. These aspects may not be the most exciting part of a BI project, but they are necessary to ensure a successful implementation.

9.1.1 Data governance: The guardian of your data assets

Data governance is like the legislation that our data needs to abide by. It sets the rules and outlines responsibilities and processes for handling data within an organization. As Thomas C. Redman, known as the "Data Doc," puts it, "Data governance is the exercise of authority and control, comprising planning, monitoring, and enforcement over the management of data assets."[55]

Data governance may seem like an abstract concept at times. Therefore, to ensure you grasp it, let's look at a simple example. We have an imaginary company called NonGov, which sells shoes online. At the end of each month, we are having trouble understanding how many sales were actually completed. Since we cannot continue having this confusion about something so basic, we start investigating where the confusion might come from.

Soon after, we learn that different departments are using different definitions of what constitutes a "sale." For instance, the sales team counts sales from the moment an order is placed. On the other hand, finance only considers it a sale when the transaction has been completed and the money is received into the company's account. By implementing data governance, we standardize this and other definitions across teams. As a result of this change, reporting and performance tracking soon become easier tasks. All our teams can now concentrate on the data and actions to be taken uniformly, rather than arguing about terminologies.

Some key aspects of data governance I would like us to review in this chapter are:

---

55. Thomas C. Redman, *Data Driven: Profiting from Your Most Important Business Asset* (Boston: Harvard Business Press, 2008).

- **Data ownership:** Clearly define who "owns" different data sets within your organization. These owners are responsible for the quality and accessibility of their data. They are also accountable for the security of their assigned data.

- **Data policies and standards:** Establish clear guidelines for data creation, storage, and usage. This includes data naming conventions, data quality standards, and data retention policies.

- **Data catalog:** Maintain a comprehensive inventory of your data assets. This helps users understand what data is available and where it comes from. It also assists users to know how data can be used.

- **Data stewardship:** Appoint data stewards responsible for implementing data governance policies. They will also act as a bridge between Information Technology (IT) teams and business users.

- **Metadata management:** Keep track of your data about data, known as metadata in other words. It helps users understand the context, lineage, and quality of the data they are working with.

According to a survey by NewVantage Partners, 98.8% of firms aspire to a data-driven culture, but only 32.4% report having achieved this goal.[56] A robust data governance framework can help bridge this gap by ensuring that data is trustworthy, accessible, and used consistently across the organization.

9.1.2 Data quality: Garbage In, Garbage Out (GIGO)

I am confident you have already internalized the principles of data quality and GIGO. However, I believe it will still be beneficial to walk through some attributes that contribute to these concepts, while we are on the subject of data management.

---

56. NewVantage Partners, "Big Data and AI Executive Survey 2021," retrieved from https://www.newvantage.com

Poor quality data can lead to flawed insights, bad decisions, and ultimately, a loss of trust in your BI system. International Business Machines (IBM) Corporation estimates that poor data quality costs the U.S. economy around $3.1 trillion per year.[57] So, how do we ensure data quality? Let's break it down:

1. **Accuracy:** Here, you need to validate if your data is correct and reliable. Regular audits and cross-checking against trusted sources can help maintain accuracy.

2. **Completeness:** Assess if you have all the necessary data. Missing data can skew your analysis and lead to incorrect conclusions.

3. **Consistency:** Cross-check if your data is consistent across different systems and departments. Inconsistent data can lead to conflicting reports and confusion.

4. **Timeliness:** Most importantly, confirm if your data is up-to-date. Outdated data can lead to missed opportunities or misguided decisions.

5. **Relevance:** Verify if the data you are collecting is actually useful for your business objectives, focus on what matters.

6. **Uniqueness:** Are you dealing with duplicated data? Duplicates can inflate numbers and lead to incorrect analysis.

Implementing a data quality management program is not a one-time effort—it is an ongoing process. As W. Edwards Deming, the father of quality management, famously said, "In God we trust; all others must bring data."[58] And I would add to that: make sure it is quality data!

Before we change gears, let me share here some strategies you can leverage for maintaining data quality:

---

57. IBM, "The Four V's of Big Data," retrieved from https://www.ibmbigdatahub.com
58. W. Edwards Deming, *Out of the Crisis* (Cambridge, MA: MIT Press, 2000).

- **Data profiling:** Regularly analyze your data to understand its content, structure, and quality. This will help identify issues before they become problems.

- **Data cleansing:** Use automated tools and manual processes to correct, standardize, and enrich your data.

- **Data validation:** Implement checks and balances to ensure data meets predefined quality criteria before it enters your BI system.

- **Continuous monitoring:** Set up automated alerts for data quality issues and regularly review data quality metrics.

- **User training:** Educate your team about the importance of data quality and their role in maintaining it. After all, data quality is everyone's responsibility.

Remember, the goal is not perfection - it is all about continuous improvement. As your BI system evolves, so should your data governance and quality management practices.

9.2 Data Security and Data Privacy

Data security and privacy are critical for efficient data management. This is evidenced by the fact that every other day we see headlines announcing data breaches and big companies being fined as a result. If you want to protect your data and keep your business away from such consequences, I would suggest securing your BI data carefully.

Let's study data security and data privacy individually to know their core components in detail:

9.2.1 Data security

You must think of all your BI data as your organization's crown jewels. Quite a simple metaphor, but you would not leave these jewels just lying around for everyone to see and grab. The same principle applies to data: do not leave it unprotected—ever.

You may feel that this chapter has adopted a pretty serious tone all of a sudden, but you probably agree that the subject of data security in BI calls for seriousness. We do not want to mess around when it comes to data security.

To begin with, let's review some essential tactics we can leverage to guarantee our data is safe:

- **Access control:** This concept can be understood in relation to the principle of "least privilege."[59] It is a minimalistic approach that aims to give users just the access they need to do their day-to-day jobs, nothing else. It is highly recommended to keep this principle in mind for everything concerned with access/permissions.

- **Data encryption:** In the discipline of data, encryption can be described as "the process of encoding information in such a way that only authorized parties can access it."[60] In simple terms, we could say that data encryption allows us to guarantee that the concerned data can only be understood and digested by pre-approved users. Data can be encrypted both 'at rest,' when it is stored, and 'in transit,' when it is being transferred.

- **Regular audits:** Always plan to conduct regular security audits to identify potential threats and vulnerabilities in your BI system. As it is often said, "your security is only as strong as your weakest link."[61]

- **Incident response plan:** Even if you are super careful and compliant with data encryption and audits, it is quite likely that some security breaches will still occur. Therefore, it is highly recommended to plan ahead and define an "incident response plan." Whenever it happens, you will want to be prepared and know how to react.

---

59. Jerome H. Saltzer and Michael D. Schroeder, "The Protection of Information in Computer Systems," *Proceedings of the IEEE* 63, no. 9 (1975): 1278-1308.

60. Christof Paar and Jan Pelzl, *Understanding Cryptography: A Textbook for Students and Practitioners* (Berlin: Springer, 2010).

61. Thomas Reid, *Essays on the Intellectual Powers of Man* (Edinburgh: John Bell, 1786).

- **Employee training:** Human error is a major contributing cause in 95% of all security breach cases—yes, 95%![62] This statistic supports the fact that whether employees act as a strong defense or a weak link in data security, depends on how they conceive security. Therefore, regular security awareness training sessions and refreshers will be crucial for success.

By following these guidelines, you will be well-equipped to avoid data breaches and bad press. However, always remember that anyone, no matter how popular or not, can be a target for security incidents. A Verizon study revealed that 43% of breaches came from small businesses.[63]

9.2.2 Data privacy

Before going any further, it is important to take a minute to cover the slight difference between data privacy and data security. The key purpose of applying data security practices is to protect ourselves and our data from unauthorized access, both internal and external. On the other hand, data privacy focuses on using data responsibly and respecting individuals' rights.

Data privacy has become such a vital and popular concept that, nowadays, we have all heard of regulations like the European General Data Protection Regulation (GDPR), or the California Consumer Privacy Act (CCPA), to name a few.

Let's explore some techniques we can use to guarantee data privacy in BI:

- **Data minimization:** Only collect and retain the data you actually need. As Ann Cavoukian, creator of Privacy by Design, states, "The collection, use, and disclosure of personal information should be limited to those

---

62. IBM Security, "Cost of a Data Breach Report 2023," retrieved from https://www.ibm.com
63. Verizon, "2023 Data Breach Investigations Report," retrieved from https://www.verizon.com

purposes that are specified to the individual at the time of collection."[64]

● **Consent management:** Before processing any data, ensure your organization has specifically received consent from relevant parties to collect and use their personal data. As part of this process, individuals will be informed about what data will be collected and how it will be used. They will also be reminded of their right to revoke this consent at any point.

● **Anonymization and pseudonymization:** Remember the data encryption concept we introduced in section 9.2.1 earlier? As an extension of data encryption, where possible and as much as possible, businesses must anonymize or pseudonymize personal data. These practices enable you to safely extract insights from your data, without compromising anybody's privacy.

● **Data subject rights:** Another frequent recommendation is to define specific processes to guide you and your team with any possible data subject requests. This includes the right to access, the right to be forgotten, and the right to data portability.

● **Assess privacy impact:** You must conduct privacy impact assessments whenever you and your team implement new BI initiatives that involve personal data. This helps identify and mitigate privacy risks early on.

A survey by Cisco found that 48% of organizations are getting significant business benefits from their privacy investments, including better agility and innovation.[65] This suggests that good privacy practices are not just about compliance—they can also offer a competitive advantage.

---

64. Ann Cavoukian, "Privacy by Design: The 7 Foundational Principles" (Information and Privacy Commissioner of Ontario, 2009).
65. Cisco, "2022 Data Privacy Benchmark Study," retrieved from https://www.cisco.com

As we near the end of this chapter, let's take a minute, recap, and truly internalize that security and privacy should be baked into our BI systems from the start, not bolted on as an afterthought. Data privacy and security are not simply technological concerns; they are a collective team responsibility that can affect our reputation and hinder our business growth potential. By ensuring strong security measures and valuing privacy, you are safeguarding not only your data but also your entire investment in BI and the future of your organization.

Chapter Summary

◆ Data governance sets the rules, responsibilities, and processes for handling data within an organization to ensure its integrity, security, and availability.

◆ Key aspects of data governance include data ownership, policies and standards, data catalogs, data stewardship, and metadata management.

◆ Data quality management ensures accuracy, completeness, consistency, timeliness, relevance, and uniqueness of data, which are crucial for reliable BI insights.

◆ Maintaining data quality involves regular data profiling, cleansing, validation, continuous monitoring, and user training.

◆ Data security is essential to protect BI data, involving access control, data encryption, regular audits, incident response planning, and employee training.

◆ Data privacy focuses on responsible data usage and respecting individuals' rights, involving practices like data minimization, consent management, anonymization, data subject rights, and privacy impact assessments.

◆ Ensuring data security and privacy helps avoid breaches, regulatory fines, and reputational damage while also providing competitive advantages and fostering trust.

Quiz

1. **What is the primary goal of data governance in BI systems?**
   a. To increase data storage
   b. To set rules, responsibilities, and processes for handling data
   c. To improve data visualization
   d. To enhance software performance

2. **What does the GIGO principle stand for?**
   a. Great Information, Great Outcomes
   b. Garbage In, Garbage Out
   c. General Information, General Output
   d. Good Input, Good Output

3. **Which of the following is a key aspect of data governance?**
   a. Data visualization
   b. Data ownership
   c. Data encryption
   d. Data integration

4. **How often should data quality management be implemented?**
   a. Once a year
   b. As a one-time effort
   c. Continuously
   d. Every five years

5. **Which principle is recommended for access control in data security?**

    a. Full access for all users

    b. Least privilege

    c. Maximum privilege

    d. No access

6. **What is the purpose of data encryption?**

    a. To speed up data processing

    b. To encode data so only authorized parties can access it

    c. To improve data visualization

    d. To organize data

7. **According to the chapter, what percentage of firms aspire to a data-driven culture but have achieved it?**

    a. 50%

    b. 75%

    c. 32.4%

    d. 98.8%

8. **What is a major contributing cause in 95% of all security breach cases?**

    a. Human error

    b. System failure

    c. External hacking

    d. Software bugs

9. **What is data minimization?**

    a. Collecting as much data as possible

    b. Only collecting and retaining data that is necessary

    c. Deleting all old data

    d. Maximizing data collection efforts

10. What does metadata management involve?

a. Creating new data

b. Keeping track of data about data

c. Deleting irrelevant data

d. Encrypting all data

Answers	1 – b	2 – b	3 – b	4 – c	5 – b
	6 – b	7 – c	8 – a	9 – b	10 – b

This page is intentionally left blank

Chapter **10**

Real-world Applications of BI

KEY LEARNING OBJECTIVES

- Explore real-world case studies to understand how BI solutions have been implemented and how they impact business outcomes.

- Explore emerging trends in BI, including artificial intelligence, machine learning, and predictive analytics.

- Understand the potential future directions of BI and how they might impact businesses in the coming years.

Welcome to the final chapter of our journey through the world of Business Intelligence! Through this book, we have covered several key concepts, foundations, techniques, and tools that may have satisfied your initial curiosity in the BI field. I hope you are motivated to continue learning and exploring this exciting world of BI.

For this last chapter, I would like us to adopt a very practical approach and bring everything we have learned together. Thus, I have gathered some real-world case studies to showcase successful BI implementations along with the learnings and benefits that originated from them. Lastly, I also want us to have a sneak peek into the future and explore some trends that have emerged during the past few years and are already shaping the future of BI practices.

10.1 Case Studies: Successful BI Implementations

While we have already seen some real-world examples throughout the book, let's utilize this section as a practical recap to strengthen the knowledge and foundations you have acquired so far in the book. Therefore, we will focus on two case studies providing tangible evidence of how these popular companies from different sectors have utilized BI. We will understand how they improved services for their clientele and outperformed their competition with BI.

10.1.1 Ubisoft - Gaming industry

For our first example, let's take a closer look at Ubisoft, the French video game giant, who over the past decades has published popular titles like Assassin's Creed and Just Dance. While their efficient use of BI has not contributed to their popularity, there is a significant amount that we can learn from them in this regard.

Ubisoft has implemented a comprehensive BI system and culture that consistently focuses on learning from player feedback and behavior analysis. To achieve this, they collect and analyze data from diverse sources such as game performance, player behavior, and social platforms. From these sources, they extract insights that enable them to make data-driven decisions and transform multiple elements of their business:

- **Game development optimization:** Ubisoft has mastered the utilization of data to improve its games. By analyzing player behavior data, Ubisoft can determine which game characteristics are performing well and which are confusing players. Their widely acclaimed game "Assassin's Creed Odyssey" is a perfect illustration of this.

When they analyzed data generated by players interacting with the game, Ubisoft discovered they were particularly enjoying the "dialogue choice" feature. Spotting that trend, they logically and rightly made sure to roll it out in future games, giving fans more of what they love.

- **Personalized gaming experiences:** Ubisoft has also benefited from the power of BI to create what are called, "personalized in-game experiences." Once again, they tapped into the technology and culture centered around constantly evaluating players' data. Using this information, they were able to adjust the game experience and complexity in real-time for each player, based on their proficiency and choices.

- **Predictive analytics for game launch:** Here is another concept introduced in this book that you are already familiar with. BI tools have given Ubisoft the edge when predicting how successful a game launch will be.

  They analyze past launches, keep an eye on market trends, and crunch the numbers on pre-orders. Similar to the predictive analytics case studies we covered in Chapter Five, with all that gathered data, Ubisoft can forecast sales and fine-tune its marketing strategies to ensure they hit the ground running.

- **Customer support enhancement:** Their BI-oriented culture approach does not just stop at gameplay. Ubisoft's BI system keeps a very close watch on customer support tickets, identifying common issues so they can nip problems in the bud and enhance overall game quality. By being proactive in this field, they are not just fixing bugs but also consistently building a better gaming experience for their users.

The impact of these BI-powered initiatives has been largely significant for Ubisoft's performance over time as reflected in their annual earnings report. From their report for the first half of 2023-24,[66] we can extract the following insights:

- The company highlights that "The Crew® 2" achieved *"exceptional engagement with a record month in terms of Monthly Active Users (MAUs), contributing to record franchise quarter activity."*

- This data-based approach has also enabled them to use their resources more efficiently, as they report a 7% reduction in their year-over-year (YoY) fixed costs. This seems to be a modest reduction but translates to a savings of €65 million.

- Following up on what we mentioned earlier about their use of predictive techniques for game launches, Ubisoft also reported a *"Strong player reception with franchise record unit sell through, consumer spending and season pass adoption rate on the opening week"* for "The Crew Motorfest."

10.1.2 Zillow - Real-estate industry

Switching to a very different industry, let's explore how Zillow Group, a well-known real estate company in the US, has been leveraging a BI-centered framework to redefine how people buy, sell, and rent properties.

Throughout this example, you will notice how their approach is to introduce and adopt BI in every aspect of their business; from how they perform house valuations, to the way they adjust property recommendations to each of their clients:

- **Zestimate® and predictive analytics:** At the core of Zillow's BI strategy is the Zestimate®, an automated tool for estimating home values. As you may have guessed already, this tool is powered by multiple machine-learning algorithms. These algorithms consistently evaluate thousands of internal and external data points such as

---

66. Ubisoft, "Ubisoft First-Half 2024 Earnings Report," retrieved from https://staticctf.ubisoft.com

property characteristics, market trends, and comparable sales nearby. As a result, in 2024 Zillow proudly reported a very impressive median error rate of less than 2%.

- **Personalized property recommendations:** Similar to Ubisoft, teams at Zillow also evaluate user behavior data such as search history, saved/shared homes, and viewing patterns. By doing this, they are empowered to generate personalized property recommendations which logically convert into higher user engagement rates and successful transactions.

- **Market trend analysis:** By crunching massive amounts of real estate data, Zillow offers valuable market insights to consumers and industry professionals alike. Their BI tools help predict market trends, enabling buyers and sellers to make more informed decisions.

- **Operational efficiency:** Zillow also uses BI to fine-tune its internal processes. For example, they analyze customer service data to pinpoint common issues and enhance support. Predictive analytics further helps them optimize marketing spend across various channels.

Zillow's BI-driven strategies have had a profound impact. In their Q4 2023 shareholder letter,[67] they reported being "the most visited rentals platform, with average unique visitors up double digits YoY in Q4." Moreover, the usage of their "super app" called Zillow is "more than three times that of its nearest competitor." Their ability to harness BI for market insights has cemented Zillow's reputation as a key player in real estate.

---

67. Zillow Group, "Zillow Q423 Shareholders Letter," retrieved from https://s24. q4cdn.com

10.2 Emerging Trends and Future Directions

We have now arrived at the last layover of our BI journey, and I think it is the perfect time to reflect on what is currently trending and upcoming for the world of business intelligence.

10.2.1 Artificial Intelligence and machine learning: The power duo

The dynamic duo of Artificial Intelligence (AI) and Machine Learning (ML) currently has the entire world's attention. Keeping it relevant for this book, I will concentrate on the integration of AI and ML into BI systems.

As AI continues to evolve and improve practically on a daily basis, we are already witnessing systems that can not only crunch numbers, but also comprehend the context behind them. These systems learn from past decisions and make predictions that at times, feel almost terrifyingly accurate.

For example, today we have access to a vast suite of BI systems that automate and streamline reporting processes. Businesses can report what happened last quarter with descriptive and diagnostic analytics, provide predictions for the following quarter's performance with predictive analytics, and derive suggestions of strategies based on that context with prescriptive analytics.

Thus, with the help of AI and ML, we can interact with technology that combines the four types of data analytics we have covered in this book.

According to a report by Gartner, in 2025, AI will be the top category driving infrastructure decisions in BI.[68] So, if you aren't already thinking about incorporating AI and ML into your BI strategy, now is the time to start.

---

68. Gartner, "Top Strategic Technology Trends for 2024," retrieved from https://www.gartner.com

10.2.2 Augmented analytics: BI for everyone

Next up is a trend that is making BI more accessible to everyone in an organization: Augmented Analytics. Here, AI and ML are leveraged to automate processes like data preparation, insight discovery, and insight sharing. This way, the practice of BI becomes a lot less technical, allowing more users to benefit from its power.

The "Augmented Analytics Market" report[69] predicts that by 2026 the compound annual growth rate (CAGR) of the augmented analytics market will reach 31.2%. This means more people will be able to leverage data insights, even if they do not have a background in data science or statistics.

10.2.3 Real-time BI: Access to latest updates

Remember when getting last month's sales figures data by the end of this month felt fast? Well, in today's business world, that is practically ancient history. Today, real-time BI is the new name of the game.

Real-time BI systems are capable of consuming, handling, and evaluating data concurrently. This allows businesses to respond immediately to changes instead of waiting days or weeks. Picture an online marketplace that can change prices instantly according to competitors' movements or a factory that can forecast and stop equipment breakdowns before they happen.

A study commissioned by KX[70] found that 90% of businesses are planning to increase their investment in real-time analytics capabilities. So if you want to stay competitive, real-time BI should be on your radar.

69. Research and Markets, "Global Augmented Analytics Market Report and Forecast 2023-2028," retrieved from https://www.researchandmarkets.com

70. KX, "Five Steps to the Microsecond Mindset," retrieved from https://kx.com

10.2.4 Data storytelling: Once upon a time, there was a bar chart…

It is not enough anymore to just present data—you need to weave it into a compelling narrative that engages your audience and drives action. As introduced in Chapter Seven, data storytelling combines data visualization with narrative techniques to explain what is happening, why it matters, and what should be done about it. It is about making data accessible and actionable for everyone, not just the data experts.

According to Gartner, in 2025, data stories will be the most widespread way of consuming analytics.[71] So start brushing up on your storytelling skills—your data has tales to tell.

10.2.5 Edge analytics: Bringing BI to the edge

To understand this concept, let me ask you a question. How many people do you know who do not use a smartphone, smartwatch, or digital assistant? I am sure your answer will be very close to none. This phenomenon is the result of a vast proliferation of Internet of Things (IoT) devices. But why is this relevant here? Because of all that phenomenon, the world is constantly generating and interchanging data, at a speed never seen before. And as promising or overwhelming as this might sound, it has also created a new challenge. Transferring all this data back to a centralized location is no longer a practical or efficient approach.

This is where edge analytics comes into play. This technology enables organizations to process data directly at the "edge" of the network, close to where it is generated. This could be on the IoT device itself, or a nearby server. The benefits? Faster processing times, reduced bandwidth usage, and improved data privacy and security.

---

71. Gartner, "4 Data Analytics Trends CFOs Can't Afford to Ignore," retrieved from https://www.gartner.com

As we conclude this journey through BI trends, I would urge you to always remember that the realm of business intelligence is ever-evolving, and perhaps so should we. What is cutting-edge today, may become common practice tomorrow. The key is not to let this intimidate us, but rather to inspire us to stay curious, keep learning, and consistently search for new ways of using data to move our business and projects forward.

You never know, in a few years, you could be the one leading the way and setting trends in BI. In the end, each BI revolution began with an individual navigating data and thinking, *"There must be a better way to do this!"* So go forth, BI enthusiasts, and may your data always be insightful!

Chapter Summary

◆ Artificial intelligence and machine learning are increasingly integrated into BI, enabling automated reporting, predictions, and strategy suggestions.

◆ Augmented analytics is democratizing BI by using AI to automate data preparation, insight discovery, and sharing. This makes data insights accessible to non-experts as well.

◆ Real-time BI allows businesses to react instantly to changes, with increasing investments in real-time analytics.

◆ Data storytelling combines data visualization with narrative techniques to make data more engaging and actionable. It is expected to be the most common way of consuming analytics in 2025.

◆ Edge analytics processes data closer to where it is generated, offering benefits like faster processing, reduced bandwidth usage, and improved data privacy.

Quiz

1. **What key feature of AI and Machine Learning drives their integration into BI systems?**
   a. Ability to process data offline
   b. Capability to automate and learn from data
   c. Cost efficiency
   d. Compatibility with all BI tools

2. **What is the expected impact of Augmented Analytics by 2026 according to the "Augmented Analytics Market" report?**
   a. Decrease in BI tool usage
   b. Increase in manual data processing
   c. 31.2% CAGR growth in the market
   d. Decline in AI integration

3. **What advantage does real-time BI offer to businesses?**
   a. Delayed data processing
   b. Historical data analysis only
   c. Instant reaction to changes as they happen
   d. Reduces the need for data security

4. **What trend combines data visualization with narrative techniques to explain data?**
   a. Augmented analytics
   b. Real-time BI
   c. Edge analytics
   d. Data storytelling

5. **Which technology is closely associated with processing data at the edge of a network?**

   a. Cloud computing

   b. Real-time BI

   c. Edge analytics

   d. Augmented analytics

6. **How does Ubisoft use BI to enhance customer support?**

   a. By analyzing customer support tickets to identify common issues

   b. By using AI to replace human support

   c. By offering 24/7 live chat only

   d. By automating all customer interactions

7. **What benefit does Zillow's BI-driven market trend analysis provide?**

   a. Automates customer service

   b. Helps buyers and sellers make informed decisions

   c. Eliminates the need for real estate agents

   d. Guarantees property sales

8. **What future trend in BI is expected to have the most widespread impact in 2025 according to Gartner?**

   a. Data storytelling

   b. Manual data entry

   c. Paper-based reporting

   d. Traditional market research

9. **What is a key benefit of edge analytics in BI?**

    a. Reduced processing time and improved data privacy

    b. Increased bandwidth usage

    c. Delayed data analysis

    d. Centralized data storage

10. **How has Ubisoft benefited from predictive analytics in game launches?**

    a. By eliminating all marketing expenses

    b. By accurately forecasting sales and fine-tuning marketing strategies

    c. By reducing game development time to zero

    d. By focusing only on old game data

Answers	1 – b	2 – c	3 – c	4 – d	5 – a
	6 – a	7 – b	8 – a	9 – a	10 – b

Case Study **1**

Transforming Inventory Management in Retail

Overview

Managing inventory is a critical aspect of retail that goes beyond logistics. It directly influences customer satisfaction and profitability. RetailCo, a US-based chain with over 500 stores, faced a recurring yet costly challenge; ensuring that essential products were consistently available while avoiding the pitfalls of overstocking or running out of key items. This case study explores how RetailCo adopted Business Intelligence (BI) to address these issues and drive both operational improvements and financial growth.

The Difficulty

RetailCo's inventory challenges were complex, affecting both operations and customer satisfaction:

Variations between locations: Some stores were swamped with excess merchandise, while others regularly experienced shortages of sought-after products, irritating shoppers.

Extra expenses: Overstock led to increased storage costs and regular write-offs for outdated items.

Missed chances: Delayed insights led to missed sales opportunities, with popular products frequently out of stock.

The Answer

Resolute in its goal to update its strategies, RetailCo implemented a state-of-the-art BI platform that fit perfectly with its current systems. The resolution developed in the following essential stages:

Centralized data integration: The BI system gathered information from Point of Sale (POS) systems, vendor records, and past sales patterns, forming a cohesive inventory perspective.

Demand prediction: Predictive analysis anticipated future demand by considering seasonality, regional tastes, and market trends.

Dynamic dashboards: Live dashboards enabled managers to monitor inventory levels, foresee shortages, and act proactively.

Automated alerts: Personalized notifications identified urgent inventory problems, allowing prompt measures to replenish or reallocate items.

The Effect

RetailCo's change was rapid and significant:

Inventory precision: Stock discrepancies decreased by 40%, guaranteeing a more reliable customer experience.

Cost efficiency: The business achieved annual savings of $2 million by optimizing inventory levels and minimizing waste.

Revenue expansion: Enhanced access to best-selling items resulted in a 15% rise in revenue.

Discussion Questions

1. What additional BI capabilities could help RetailCo refine its inventory management further?

2. How can smaller retailers replicate RetailCo's success on a limited budget?

3. What are the potential risks of relying heavily on predictive analytics for inventory decisions?

Case Activity

Using sample retail data, create a basic visualization that highlights trends in sales and inventory. Identify actionable insights that could improve inventory planning.

Case Study **2**

Optimizing Patient Care Through BI

Overview

As it is fair to expect, the healthcare industry demands a delicate balance of efficiency and precision, where even minor delays can significantly impact patient outcomes.

HealthMy Hospital, a 250-bed facility in New York City, was grappling with increasing pressure to enhance patient care while managing operational costs. By implementing a tailored BI system, HealthMy successfully turned these challenges into opportunities, becoming a leader in data-driven healthcare solutions.

The Difficulty

HealthMy's struggles reflected common issues faced by healthcare providers:

Overcrowded emergency rooms (ERs): Persistent ER wait times frustrated patients and overburdened resources.

Inefficient resource utilization: Misaligned staff schedules and equipment allocation often hampered timely care.

Limited data visibility: Without real-time data, decision-making was reactive rather than proactive.

The Answer

HealthMy adopted a comprehensive BI platform, customized for the complexities of healthcare. Key initiatives included:

Enhanced data accessibility: The BI system integrated Electronic Health Records (EHRs), staffing schedules, and patient feedback into a single interface.

Predictive analytics: Advanced models predicted patient admission patterns, enabling better resource planning.

Operational dashboards: Real-time views of bed occupancy, ER wait times, and staff availability supported dynamic decision-making.

Outcome tracking: The system monitored patient outcomes, identifying trends and areas for intervention.

The Effect

The results were transformative:

Reduced wait times: ER wait times dropped by 30%, improving patient experiences and throughput.

Better resource allocation: Efficiency in staff scheduling and equipment usage improved by 20%.

Improved patient outcomes: Targeted interventions for high-risk patients reduced readmissions by 15%.

Cost savings: Operational efficiencies saved the hospital $1.5 million annually.

Discussion Questions

1. How can HealthMy expand its BI capabilities to address other areas of care?

2. What safeguards should be in place to ensure patient data privacy?

3. How might BI tools help smaller clinics or rural hospitals with fewer resources?

Case Activity

Draft a mock patient flow diagram using BI insights to optimize ER operations. Identify potential bottlenecks and propose data-driven solutions.

References

Chapter 1

1. Codd, E. F. "A Relational Model of Data for Large Shared Data Banks." *Communications of the ACM* 13, no. 6 (1970): 377-387.
2. Davenport, Thomas H., and Jeanne G. Harris. *Competing on Analytics: The New Science of Winning.* Harvard Business Review Press, 2007.
3. Devens, Richard M. *Cyclopædia of Commercial and Business Anecdotes.* New York: D. Appleton and Company, 1865.
4. Dresner, Howard. "Business Intelligence: A Set of Concepts and Methodologies to Improve Decision Making in Business through Fact-based Support Systems." Gartner Group, 1989.
5. Few, Stephen. *Information Dashboard Design: The Effective Visual Communication of Data.* O'Reilly Media, 2006.
6. Inmon, W. H. *Building the Data Warehouse.* New York: John Wiley & Sons, Inc., 1992.
7. Kimball, Ralph, and Margy Ross. *The Data Warehouse Toolkit: The Complete Guide to Dimensional Modeling.* New York: John Wiley & Sons, 2002.
8. Power, D. J. *Decision Support, Analytics, and Business Intelligence.* Business Expert Press, 2013.
9. Russom, Philip. *Big Data Analytics.* TDWI Best Practices Report, Fourth Quarter 2011.

Chapter 2

1. Amazon Web Services (AWS). n.d. *AWS Documentation.* Retrieved from https://aws.amazon.com
2. Gartner. n.d. "Reports on Business Intelligence and Data Analytics." *Gartner Inc.* Retrieved from https://www.gartner.com/
3. Google Cloud Platform (GCP). n.d. *Google Cloud Documentation.* Retrieved from https://cloud.google.com/docs
4. Inmon, W. H. 2005. *Building the Data Warehouse.* 4th ed. Wiley.
5. Kimball, R., and Ross, M. 2013. *The Data Warehouse Toolkit: The Definitive Guide to Dimensional Modeling.* 3rd ed. Wiley.
6. Marz, N., and Warren, J. 2015. *Big Data: Principles and Best Practices of Scalable Real-Time Data Systems.* Manning Publications.
7. Microsoft Azure. n.d. *Azure Documentation.* Retrieved from https://docs.microsoft.com
8. Sherman, R. 2014. *Cloud Data Management and Warehousing: Complete Guide.* Technics Publications.

Chapter 3

1. Coursera. *"BI Tools: The Complete Guide."* Retrieved from https://www.coursera.org
2. DataCamp. *"Top Business Intelligence Tools."* Retrieved from https://www.datacamp.com
3. Gartner. *"Analytics and Business Intelligence Platforms Reviews and Ratings."* Retrieved from https://www.gartner.com
4. SelectHub. *"Business Intelligence Tools."* Retrieved from https://www.selecthub.com

Chapter 4

1. Amplitude. "What is Diagnostic Analytics?" Retrieved from https://amplitude.com
2. Chen, H., Chiang, R. H. L., & Storey, V. C. (2012). "Business Intelligence and Analytics: From Big Data to Big Impact." *MIS Quarterly*, 36(4), 1165-1188. Retrieved from https://www.jstor.org
3. Davenport, T. H., & Harris, J. G. (2007). *Competing on Analytics: The New Science of Winning*. Harvard Business Review Press. Retrieved from https://hbr.org
4. Devens, R. M. (1865). *Cyclopædia of Commercial and Business Anecdotes*. New York: D. Appleton and Company.
5. Eckerson, Wayne W. *Performance Dashboards: Measuring, Monitoring, and Managing Your Business*. Hoboken, NJ: John Wiley & Sons, 2010.
6. Few, Stephen. *Information Dashboard Design: The Effective Visual Communication of Data*. O'Reilly Media, 2006.
7. Gartner. "Descriptive Analytics." Retrieved from Gartner Glossary.
8. Harvard Business School Online. (2020, October 21). "What is Diagnostic Analytics?" Retrieved from Business Insights.
9. Hoffman, Sean Tierney. "Blank Canvas Syndrome." Retrieved from https://grid7.com
10. JMP. "What is Correlation? Correlation Coefficient." Retrieved from https://www.jmp.com
11. Jaspersoft. "What is Descriptive Analytics?" Retrieved from https://www.jaspersoft.com
12. KnowledgeHut. "Descriptive Analytics: What It Is and Why It Matters." Retrieved from https://www.knowledgehut.com
13. Montgomery, D. C. (2012). *Introduction to Statistical Quality Control*. Wiley. Retrieved from https://www.wiley.com
14. Provost, F., & Fawcett, T. (2013). *Data Science for Business: What You Need to Know about Data Mining and Data-Analytic Thinking*. O'Reilly Media.
15. Redman, T. C. (2013). *Data Driven: Profiting from Your Most Important Business Asset*. Harvard Business Review Press. Retrieved from https://hbr.org
16. Sallam, Rita L., et al. (2020). "Magic Quadrant for Analytics and Business Intelligence Platforms." *Gartner Research*.

17. Shmueli, G., Patel, N. R., & Bruce, P. C. (2010). *Data Mining for Business Intelligence: Concepts, Techniques, and Applications in Microsoft Office Excel with XLMiner.* Wiley. Retrieved from https://www.wiley.com

18. Tableau Software. *Visual Analysis Best Practices: Simple Techniques for Making Every Data Visualization Useful and Beautiful.* Retrieved from https://www.tableau.com

19. Turban, Efraim, Ramesh Sharda, Dursun Delen, and David King. (2011). *Business Intelligence: A Managerial Approach.* 2nd ed. Upper Saddle River, NJ: Prentice Hall.

Chapter 5

1. Bregman, Steven. "How Data Analytics Emerged as a Competitive Advantage for the Mercedes-AMG Petronas Formula One Team." TIBCO Blog, August 27, 2020. https://www.tibco.com

2. DataCamp. "Classification in Machine Learning." DataCamp Blog. Retrieved from https://www.datacamp.com

3. GeeksforGeeks. "Pros and Cons of Decision Tree Regression in Machine Learning." Retrieved from https://www.geeksforgeeks.org

4. GeeksforGeeks. "Python | Decision Tree Regression Using Sklearn." Retrieved from https://www.geeksforgeeks.org

5. Google Cloud. "What is Predictive Analytics?" Retrieved from https://cloud.google.com

6. Met Office. "Predicting Extreme Weather." Retrieved from https://www.metoffice.gov.uk

7. Saunders, Ed. "Meet the IntelligentEngine Taking Predictive Engine Maintenance to the Next Level." Aircraft IT MRO, September 17, 2020. https://www.aircraftit.com

8. Tran, James. "Amazon Data Science Interview Guide." DataLemur (blog). Retrieved from https://datalemur.com

Chapter 6

1. Amplitude. "What Is Prescriptive Analytics?" Retrieved from https://amplitude.com

2. Bertsimas, Dimitris, and John N. Tsitsiklis. Introduction to Linear Optimization. Belmont, MA: Athena Scientific, 1997.

3. Bonabeau, Eric. "Agent-based Modeling: Methods and Techniques for Simulating Human Systems." Proceedings of the National Academy of Sciences 99, no. 3 (2002): 7280-7287.

4. Clemen, Robert T., and Terence Reilly. Making Hard Decisions with DecisionTools Suite. Mason, OH: Cengage Learning, 2013.

5. Dantzig, George B. Linear Programming and Extensions. Princeton, NJ: Princeton University Press, 1963.

6.   Du, D.-Z., and P.M. Pardalos, eds. Handbook of Combinatorial Optimization. 2nd ed. Dordrecht: Kluwer Academic Publishers, 1998. "Optimization Applications in the Airline Industry." Retrieved from https://sites.rutgers.edu

7.   Emerj Artificial Intelligence Research. "Artificial Intelligence at Procter & Gamble." Retrieved from https://emerj.com

8.   Few, Stephen. Show Me the Numbers: Designing Tables and Graphs to Enlighten. Burlingame, CA: Analytics Press, 2012.

9.   INFORMS. "WSC 2024 Keynotes - Simulation for Disney Parks and Experiences." Retrieved from https://meetings.informs.org

10. Law, Averill M., and W. David Kelton. Simulation Modeling and Analysis. 4th ed. New York: McGraw-Hill, 2000.

11. Nocedal, Jorge, and Stephen J. Wright. Numerical Optimization. 2nd ed. New York: Springer, 2006.

12. Pfeffer, Jeffrey, and Robert I. Sutton. The Knowing-Doing Gap: How Smart Companies Turn Knowledge into Action. Boston: Harvard Business School Press, 2000.

13. Raiffa, Howard. Decision Analysis: Introductory Lectures on Choices Under Uncertainty. Reading, MA: Addison-Wesley, 1968.

14. Rubinstein, Reuven Y., and Dirk P. Kroese. Simulation and the Monte Carlo Method. 2nd ed. Hoboken, NJ: John Wiley & Sons, 2016.

15. Schwartz, Peter. The Art of the Long View: Planning for the Future in an Uncertain World. New York: Doubleday, 1991.

16. UPS. "UPS to Enhance ORION with Continuous Delivery Route Optimization." Retrieved from https://about.ups.com

Chapter 7

1.   Cairo, Alberto. *The Functional Art: An Introduction to Information Graphics and Visualization*. Berkeley, CA: New Riders, 2012.

2.   Cairo, Alberto. *The Truthful Art: Data, Charts, and Maps for Communication*. Berkeley, CA: New Riders, 2016.

3.   Eckerson, Wayne W. *Performance Dashboards: Measuring, Monitoring, and Managing Your Business*. 2nd ed. Hoboken, NJ: John Wiley & Sons, 2010.

4.   Few, Stephen. *Information Dashboard Design: The Effective Visual Communication of Data*. Sebastopol, CA: O'Reilly Media, 2006.

5.   Few, Stephen. *Information Dashboard Design: Displaying Data for At-a-Glance Monitoring*. 2nd ed. Analytics Press, 2013.

6.   Few, Stephen. *Now You See It: Simple Visualization Techniques for Quantitative Analysis*. Analytics Press, 2009.

7.   Few, Stephen. *Show Me the Numbers: Designing Tables and Graphs to Enlighten*. 2nd ed. Burlingame, CA: Analytics Press, 2012.

8.   Knaflic, Cole Nussbaumer. *Storytelling with Data: A Data Visualization Guide for Business Professionals*. Hoboken, NJ: John Wiley & Sons, 2015.

9.   Munzner, Tamara. *Visualization Analysis and Design*. Boca Raton, FL: CRC Press, 2014.

10. Stone, Maureen. *A Field Guide to Digital Color*. CRC Press, 2003.

11. Tufte, Edward R. *The Visual Display of Quantitative Information*. 2nd ed. Cheshire, CT: Graphics Press, 2001.

12. Ware, Colin. *Information Visualization: Perception for Design*. 3rd ed. Morgan Kaufmann, 2012.

13. Ware, Colin. *Information Visualization: Perception for Design*. 4th ed. Cambridge, MA: Morgan Kaufmann, 2020.

14. Wexler, Steve, Jeffrey Shaffer, and Andy Cotgreave. *The Big Book of Dashboards: Visualizing Your Data Using Real-World Business Scenarios*. Hoboken, NJ: John Wiley & Sons, 2017.

15. Wong, Dona M. *The Wall Street Journal Guide to Information Graphics: The Dos and Don'ts of Presenting Data, Facts, and Figures*. W. W. Norton & Company, 2010.

16. Yau, Nathan. *Data Points: Visualization That Means Something*. John Wiley & Sons, 2013.

17. Yau, Nathan. *Visualize This: The FlowingData Guide to Design, Visualization, and Statistics*. Indianapolis, IN: Wiley Publishing, 2011.

18. Yuk, Mico, and Stephanie Diamond. *Data Visualization For Dummies*. Hoboken, NJ: John Wiley & Sons, 2014.

Chapter 8

1. Collier, Ken. *Agile Analytics: A Value-Driven Approach to Business Intelligence and Data Warehousing*. Boston: Addison-Wesley Professional, 2011.

2. Kotter, John P. *Leading Change*. Boston: Harvard Business School Press, 1996.

Chapter 9

1. Batini, Carlo, Cinzia Cappiello, Chiara Francalanci, and Andrea Maurino. "Methodologies for Data Quality Assessment and Improvement." ACM Computing Surveys 41, no. 3 (2009): 1-52.

2. General Data Protection Regulation (GDPR). "Regulation (EU) 2016/679 of the European Parliament and of the Council." Retrieved from https://eur-lex.europa.eu

3. Khatri, Vijay, and Carol V. Brown. "Designing Data Governance." Communications of the ACM 53, no. 1 (2010): 148-152.

4. National Institute of Standards and Technology (NIST). "NIST Cybersecurity Framework." Retrieved from https://www.nist.gov

5. Ponemon Institute. "The Human Factor in Data Protection." Retrieved from https://www.ponemon.org

6. Wang, Richard Y., and Diane M. Strong. "Beyond Accuracy: What Data Quality Means to Data Consumers." Journal of Management Information Systems 12, no. 4 (1996): 5-33.

7.   Yeoh, William, and Andy Koronios. "Critical Success Factors for Business
     Intelligence Systems." Journal of Computer Information Systems 50, no. 3 (2010):
     23-32.

Chapter 10

1.   LinkedIn. "Ubisoft's Pioneering Achievements in Gaming Research." LinkedIn
     Pulse. Retrieved from https://www.linkedin.com
2.   Ubisoft. "Making Better Gaming Happen: Discover the EMEA CRC." Ubisoft
     Careers. Retrieved from https://www.ubisoft.com
3.   Zillow. "Zestimate®: Real Estate & Homes for Sale." Zillow. Retrieved from
     https://www.zillow.com
4.   Zillow Group. "Quarterly Results." Zillow Group Investors. Retrieved from
     https://investors.zillowgroup.com

NOTES

www.ingramcontent.com/pod-product-compliance
Lightning Source LLC
Chambersburg PA
CBHW060255220326
41598CB00027B/4116